Randy Johnson's
Power Pitching

RANDY JOHNSON'S POWER PITCHING

The Big Unit's Secrets to Domination, Intimidation, and Winning

RANDY JOHNSON

with Jim Rosenthal

Foreword by NOLAN RYAN

THREE RIVERS PRESS · NEW YORK

Published by Three Rivers Press, New York, New York.
Member of the Crown Publishing Group, a division of Random House, Inc.
www.randomhouse.com

The photographs on pages 3, 4, 5, 11, and 68 are from the author's personal collection. The photographs on pages 114 and 121 are used by permission of Barry Gossage. The photographs on page 28 and 109 are used by permission of PhotoFile.

THREE RIVERS PRESS and the Tugboat design are registered trademarks of Random House, Inc.

Printed in the United States of America

Design by Barbara Sturman

Library of Congress Cataloging-in-Publication Data
Johnson, Randy, 1963–
    Randy Johnson's power pitching : the big unit's secrets to domination, intimidation, and winning / Randy Johnson with Jim Rosenthal.—1st ed.
1. Pitching (Baseball). 2. Johnson, Randy, 1963–. I. Title: Power pitching.
II. Rosenthal, Jim. III. Title.
    GV871 .J65   2003
    796.352'22—dc21   2002012315

ISBN 1-4000-4739-0

10 9 8 7 6 5 4 3 2 1

First Edition

To my father, Bud Johnson, for all his tireless efforts to help me reach my full potential as a pitcher and as a person. I'm forever grateful for his love and support.

Acknowledgments

This book could not have been written without the help of the following people and organizations:

Nolan Ryan;

Lisa Johnson;

Alan Nero and the management team at CSMG
(www.csmgsports.com);

Casey Wilcox and the media relations department of the
2002 World Champion Arizona Diamondbacks;

Damian Miller;

Tom DiPace;

Pete Fornatale, Steve Ross, and Dorianne Steele at Crown;

Shari Wenk;

Billy Witter,

Colorado Rockies media relations department;

Larry Walker;

Mark Connor;

Tom House;

Brett Fischer (www.fischer-sports.com);

Rochelle Smith, Los Angeles Dodgers;

and special thanks to the Fairmont Scottsdale Princess.

Contents

Foreword

I first met Randy Johnson many years ago when he was still pitching with the Seattle Mariners and I was pitching with the Texas Rangers.

Randy approached me on the field one day and wanted to know if I had a few minutes to visit with him. He told me about some of his frustrations with the way things were going, and I felt that he was on the verge of putting it all together; he only needed to be consistent with his delivery.

Randy had a tendency to spin out on his heel as he was delivering the pitch. He wasn't as directional toward home plate as was necessary to throw strikes consistently. After making that one significant change in his mechanics—that he land on the ball of his foot instead of his heel—Randy developed into one of the best control pitchers in baseball.

We also talked about his approach to pitching, and about his mound presence. Ten years later he has become the most dominating pitcher in the game today.

Randy is extremely focused and an aggressive competitor, a great improvement since I met with him back in the '92 season. He is very dedicated to his physical conditioning regimen, and is working hard to make the most of the God-given talent he's been blessed with.

Randy came to me because he was looking to improve his control. It helps to have an open mind about applying new ideas to your repertoire as a pitcher. That's what Randy's book is all about.

As a pitcher—both when I was starting my career and after I became an established major leaguer—I was always interested in checking out new information to see if it was applicable to me. It's vital always to keep an open mind and look to improve and get better. Randy is living proof that it takes hard work and dedication to maximize potential. But he was the first to admit that he didn't know everything, and that he needed help to perform at his best.

During my pitching career, I had to be aggressive and competitive on the mound. That's not at all my personality off the field. Randy is the same way—an intimidating presence on the mound and a mild-mannered, friendly family man off the field.

I honestly believe that all pitchers—not just power pitchers—need to be aggressive. That's one of the key points I tried to convey to Randy from day one in our discussions about the art of pitching. My attitude was that I was not going to stand out there and just let those guys hit the ball. I was going to make the other team strain to beat me—I wasn't going to just feed them the ball and let fly.

Randy applies that principle of mental toughness to his mound presence, and the results speak for themselves. His numbers are phenomenal. He has been the biggest impact pitcher in the major leagues over the last ten years. In fact he is one of the best pitchers in the history of the game of baseball. And I'm honored to be able to say that our paths crossed, that we learned from each other, and that I'm a better person for knowing Randy Johnson—the ultimate power pitcher of his generation.

NOLAN RYAN

Alvin, Texas
May 2002

Randy Johnson's Power Pitching

1

THE EDUCATION OF A POWER PITCHER

*T*he goal of this book is to teach you how to be a complete pitcher. I want to share my experience to help you fulfill your full potential.

Many people assume that success came easy to me. After all, I'm a power pitcher with pinpoint control, four Cy Young Awards, and a World Series ring. The plain truth is that I struggled at every level. I was wild and inconsistent for much of my high school, college, and minor-league pitching career.

Sure, there were fifteen-strikeout games and one-hit shutouts to keep me going. But I was just as likely to walk seven or eight batters and give up five or six runs. My mechanics were a mess. I was all over the place when I pitched, never landing in the same spot twice. My height and extremely long arms and legs made it very difficult to be compact in my delivery.

The odd thing is that no one ever taught me to be consistent with my mechanics until I was a big-league pitcher. Once I corrected a mechanical flaw in my delivery, I suddenly went from an out-of-control thrower to the control pitcher.

My whole career has been a progression. I never took success for granted. I've had to work hard for everything. And I took my lumps like everyone else.

I'm going to teach you the keys to becoming a complete pitcher—mental toughness, proper mechanics, pitch location, and proper grips and physical conditioning. But it will be up to you to put the advice into practice and turn your potential into the intangibles that make a winning pitcher.

Playing to win has always been a way of life for me. My entire career has been an ongoing process of staying focused on maximum performance.

But I want to stress right from the beginning that you cannot be successful in baseball unless your interest springs from playing the game just for the fun of it.

I've conducted many Little League clinics, and my key message to parents is to let their child enjoy the game. Let him or her progress at a natural and comfortable pace, with help from the coaches along the way. Do not put pressure on kids to take the game too seriously.

Pushing kids too hard is not going to ensure success. In fact, that's often the biggest barrier that kids face. I realize that the motives are usually positive. After all, every parent wants the best for his or her kids, but in the earliest stages of a pitcher's life, the bottom line is having fun.

My son and daughter play baseball and soccer, and I'm supportive of them in every way. But how I can evaluate whether my six-year-old son will ever play in the major leagues? For that matter, how do I know my son is even going to want to play baseball?

It's not my position to push him in that direction. My dad was a police officer, not a professional athlete. He just wanted to be supportive of my interest and passion for baseball. My mom was there to help me, too. A supportive environment will make a big difference right from the beginning.

My baseball career began at the age of seven in Livermore, California, about forty-five minutes east of Oakland. Like a lot of kids, I played imaginary baseball games, throwing a tennis ball against the garage door with tape on it in the shape of a box to simulate home plate.

My Little League debut at the age of eight.

I was ten years old and hooked on youth soccer.

It took about 200 fastballs for the nails holding the garage door in place to come undone. My dad arrived with a hammer just before the door fell off its hinges, and we both understood that it was my responsibility to pound the nails back in so I could start my imaginary game all over again.

When I played catch with my dad, he was incredibly patient and generous with his time. My control was terrible. I'd throw five or six pitches over his head, and he'd tell me, "You start getting those balls, Randy." His insistence that I do the work to retrieve those wild throws forced me to focus on improving my location.

I threw harder than all the other Little Leaguers, and I was growing up faster and taller than most of my peers. It didn't take long to sort out the top pitchers in Little League and Babe Ruth League.

Little League was fun. Babe Ruth League was also fun. At these early stages the goal is to get the feel of your pitches and start hitting your spots. I learned how to throw my first breaking ball when I was eleven years old—it was sort of a "slurve," a cross between a curve and a slider. In Babe Ruth baseball, and later in high school, I was exposed to a variety of different pitches and grips. The concept was to put a little bit of a wrinkle into my repertoire to set up my fastball.

The town of Livermore had two big high schools. All the top pitchers from my Little League and Babe Ruth teams went to Granada High School. I ended up at Livermore High.

My main competition as the best prep pitcher in the area was Kevin Trudeau, the brother of Jack Trudeau, who became the starting quarterback for the University of Illinois and went on to play in the NFL several years later.

Kevin pitched against me at every level, from Little League through high school, and I always thought of him as a better athlete than I. He was a starting quarterback in Pop Warner, and I was a one-sport athlete at that point, though I did enjoy playing soccer and tennis for fun.

We had a terrific rivalry, and I enjoyed competing against him. I would have predicted that he would be the one to go on to major-league success, but it just goes to show that hard work and dedication will pay off if you keep believing in yourself.

Above: A 14-year-old self-styled Ken Stabler-lefthanded quarterback in Pop Warner Football. *Left:* A snapshot from my American Legion years in Oakland. This Legion team (Bercovich) was made up of All-Star caliber baseball players from the Bay Area and Livermore Valley.

To become a better pitcher, I decided to develop better hand-eye coordination and competitive intensity by playing a second team sport. I picked up a basketball for the first time at the beginning of freshman year in high school, and through hard work—and with the help of my height advantage—I started for three years on the Livermore High basketball team. I was developing into an all-around athlete, and it was very gratifying to feel that I could hold my own in a sport besides baseball.

My dad was an invaluable help during this part of my life. After work, he would come to my high school baseball games and sit in the bleachers to watch me pitch. When I played on an American Legion team in Oakland, he would drive me to and from the games, two or three hours each way, two or three times per week. That was a sacrifice he was willing to make because he saw that baseball was something I was good at and enjoyed.

My dad taught me the value of hard work. He never forced me to play baseball or basketball, but once I made a commitment to do something, he was there to help and encourage me in every way possible, and the work ethic I learned from his example has helped me improve at each step of my baseball career.

PITCHING STRATEGY 101

High school is the most important developmental phase of an athlete's career. It's the first time you hear about a talented pitcher with big-league potential getting scouted. In basketball, such gifted athletes as Kobe Bryant and Tracy McGrady skipped right from high school into the pros and achieved immediate stardom.

In baseball, it is a lot tougher to make that leap. So much depends on your willingness to improve your skills. If you've been blessed with a good fastball, you must learn how to throw it for strikes. It took me a lot longer than most to figure out how to harness the power of this pitch. I attribute my slow learning curve to my height and to the mechanical problems it presents.

Think of high school as the time to get to know your strengths and weaknesses as a pitcher. Take the initiative to

I'm beginning my forward movement toward home plate. As I start to move forward, my hand has separated from the glove and I'm preparing to land on the mound with my lead leg. You must work on landing in the same spot every time you throw a pitch. Consistency is one of the keys to pitching success.

Rick Williams was another Expos pitching instructor who helped me to improve my mechanics. He worked with me on each step of the pitching motion; here, my shoulders and hips are opening up to deliver the ball.

learn about hitters and how they operate. It's simple: Your job is to throw off the timing of the hitter. How is this done?

- **By changing speeds.**
- **By hitting spots—up and away, down and away, up and in, and down and in.**

About 90 percent of the time I will throw a slider in an 0–2 or 1–2 count because it is my strikeout pitch. But if you *always* throw the same pitch in the same situation, you become too predictable. When I throw an 0–2 fastball right down the middle and I get a called third strike it is quite obvious that the hitter was not looking for that pitch.

Outsmarting a hitter is one of the gratifying aspects of pitching. When you fool him with your pitch selection, you know you've become a pitcher, and not just a guy who is throwing the ball as hard as possible without a plan or a strategy.

I'll typically work a right-handed hitter away, and then, when he's looking on the outside part of the plate, I can come in with my slider or my fastball down and in.

I have a lot of confidence in my breaking ball. I can throw it in a fastball count (2–0, 3–1, or 3–2) and get a swing and a miss because the hitter was guessing fastball. If you fall behind in the count and are forced to throw a fastball, then you'd better be able to hit your spot—and it had better be a spot that the hitter is not anticipating, or you are going to get hurt.

It is best to figure this out while you are still in high school. In the past six or seven years I've learned a great deal about pitching. That's why I've developed into a more complete pitcher late in my career. I developed into a pitcher instead of a thrower because I've taken the time to match up my knowledge of *how* to pitch with my good stuff—my fastball and slider. This combination of the mental and physical sides of the game has turned me into a dominating pitcher over the past four or five years.

It was that "good stuff," the high-velocity fastball and improving slider, that gave me hope I could play baseball past my high school years. Scouts from major-league teams started showing up during my junior year, and that routine continued almost every time I pitched as a senior.

I'm not going to tell you that this was the culmination of a dream I had when I was playing catch with my father. I enjoyed playing baseball and I knew that I had the raw talent to excel, but I wasn't one of those kids who put all his hopes into making it to the big leagues.

I remember going to the Oakland Coliseum for an Oakland A's game on Little League Day. Vida Blue, my hero and role model—he was a hard-throwing lefty like me—played on that field, and I imagined that one day perhaps I could pitch there, too.

By the end of high school, I started to consider the possibilities: As raw as I was with mechanics and control, it was beginning to seem likely that I had a career in baseball. My high school baseball coach offered encouragement, and the scouts reinforced that feeling of optimism.

The Atlanta Braves drafted me in the fourth round in June of my senior year. I was happy that a big-league organization thought so highly of my potential, but I had several options to play college baseball. I liked the idea of furthering my education while learning more about the craft of pitching.

I had scholarship offers from the University of Oklahoma, the University of Hawaii, and USC. I even had the option of

Pitching for the USC Trojans in a game at Dodger Stadium during my sophomore year.

playing both baseball and basketball at St. Mary's College in Moraga, a suburb of Oakland.

I sat down with my parents and we decided that playing collegiate basketball was not going to lead to any opportunities down the road. I had worked very hard to develop my hoop skills, and had been an All-Star in Bay Area high school tournaments, but my best chance of doing anything significant with my life still rested with throwing a baseball.

At this point I could throw a fastball well over 90 mph, and had developed the sharp-breaking slider. I had to master my control of those two pitches before I could hope to have any success at the professional level.

In the end I decided to play baseball at USC—a program with a solid reputation as a national power, and my best chance for being drafted in June of my junior year (which is when col-

I have a low three-quarter release point, and I keep my torso upright. The taller you stand—regardless of your actual height—the more downward motion you'll need in the delivery, and that will make it harder for the hitter to pick up the pitch coming out of your hand.

The legs, back, and shoulders absorb much of the force of slowing the arm down after delivering the pitch. I pitch with my upper body, but it is important to strengthen all parts of the body—especially the abdominals and lower back—to deal with the wear and tear of pitching.

I pitch with emotion. I struggled during my last season in Seattle because my emotions were taking my mind off the game. You need to stay focused, but that is easier said than done. If I had to go through the whole process of wondering when I was going to get traded, I wouldn't have allowed my emotions to become such a force, but that emotional intensity is what makes me unique.

lege baseball players are eligible to be drafted by major-league baseball teams).

I had turned down a chance to play pro ball because I wasn't ready to pitch in the minors. If I'd signed with the Braves, my entire life would have taken a different path, and I'm thankful for how things have worked out for me.

Even if you are good enough to sign right out of high school—and this applies to many young pitchers—you must evaluate where you are in your progress, and what you need to do to advance to the next level.

If my son had the opportunity to sign a major-league contract after high school, I would ask him two key questions: If baseball does not work out for you, what do you have to fall back on? Are you ready to play professional baseball right now?

The decision would be his to make, but it would be my responsibility as a father to let him know that a college education is important and will mean a lot to him whether or not he makes it in pro ball.

I enjoyed my college experience, but in terms of pitching instruction it was a setback, because I never got the one-on-one coaching that I needed to improve my mechanics. My "big discovery" and major breakthrough in refining my mechanics were still several years away.

Pitching at the college level raises the stakes even higher. The talent pool improves, and you are compared with many athletes who will eventually pitch in the majors. If things don't work out on the mound, you'll be pushed out of the way and be forced to do something else with your life. Of course, one of the advantages of going to college is that you become aware of alternative careers.

Despite my erratic control at USC, I pitched well enough

to attract the interest of the Montreal Expos. I signed a contract with a $64,000 bonus after my junior year, and I felt vindicated for waiting to turn pro. Of course, during my fourteen-year career I've made more money than I ever imagined, but money was not my motivation to sign a pro contract. If it had only been about the money, I would have started my pro career three years earlier.

THE NOLAN RYAN EXPRESS CONNECTION

My first minor-league experience was pitching for Jamestown (short-season Class A baseball) in the New York–Penn League. I was one of a group of talented young pitchers in the Montreal Expos organization, but I still had a long way to go.

Jim Fanning, director of player development for Montreal, watched me pitch two games. In the first start, I fanned fifteen batters in seven innings; in the next start I walked ten batters and gave up seven earned runs.

Fanning was wondering what was going on. As he looked at my motion, the answer became obvious; my inconsistency was a by-product of bad mechanics.

It was an up-and-down year, but I enjoyed my first taste of pro ball. I figured out how I rated against the other guys, and I knew I had more velocity; however, I still had a lot to learn about pitching, and my mechanics were still unrefined.

I survived that year (0–3 with a 5.93 ERA) and reported to West Palm Beach, Florida, to work on my mechanics and PFP (pitcher's fielding practice) drills with the Expos' roving pitching instructor, Rick Williams. I look back on the instructional league experience as the first time I had the opportunity to work one-on-one with a pitching coach to analyze my delivery.

I look back fondly on my career with Seattle. We made it to post-season play twice—
1995 and 1997—and you have to remember that when I arrived in the Pacific Northwest in
1989, the Mariners had been around twenty-two years and had never even finished with
a .500 record. I took great pleasure in the success of the Mariners in 2001. My ultimate
World Series thrill would be pitching for the Arizona Diamondbacks against the Mariners
and winning Game 7.

This is an example of the high leg kick that Nolan Ryan made famous. The point of the leg kick is to achieve ideal balance so that you can align the body to point directly toward home plate when you deliver the ball. While I was with Montreal, I was still fine-tuning my delivery. I had a tendency to fly off toward third base, and that often meant throwing balls instead of strikes.

The next season at West Palm Beach (8–7, 3.16 ERA, 133 strikeouts in 119.2 innings) was a marked improvement, but the leap to AA Jacksonville in 1987 was the biggest step in my career to date. I put together a winning record (11–8, 3.73 ERA, 162 strikeouts in 140 innings) while developing more confidence in my pitches.

Joe Kerrigan, former pitching coach for the Montreal Expos and the Boston Red Sox, worked with me at Jacksonville in 1987 and once again at Indianapolis in 1988 (8–7, 3.26 ERA, 111 strikeouts in 113.1 innings). Kerrigan was very meticulous in teaching me about body language and mound presence, and how my attitude and behavior would make me a more intimidating pitcher.

Nolan Ryan had a reputation for an intimidating mound presence; he would stare hitters down; he would glare at guys who stole bases against him. I have a tendency to stare a hitter down if he argues a called third strike. This game is tough enough without hitters arguing balls and strikes with the umpire. The hitter gets to enjoy his tour around the bases after hitting a home run, so why should he also get to argue whether or not I punched him out on a "borderline" pitch?

THE ART OF PITCHING INSIDE

Another part of the intimidation factor that defines power pitching is the need to pitch inside—always a high priority for Nolan during his career, and another pitching tool that Joe Kerrigan hammered into my head. I'm a firm believer that you have to establish that you own the inside part of the plate. If you only pitch to the outside, you are telling the hitter that

In my early days with the Montreal Expos organization, I was one of a group of talented young pitchers, but my inconsistent mechanics kept me from moving quickly to the big leagues. I struggled through my first season of pro baseball in the New York–Penn League with an 0–3 record and a 5.93 ERA. But working on my mechanics in the Expos instructional league helped me improve every aspect of my game.

he owns the inside, and he can lean in over the plate and do plenty of damage.

More home runs are hit from the belt/middle than belt/in. Hitters will get jammed when you pitch inside, and they won't be able to drive the ball with as much success. Of course, this will vary from hitter to hitter. But it is your responsibility to take ownership of the inside part of the plate.

A hitter wants to extend his arms—that's where his power comes from. If you are throwing the ball outside all the time, you're looking for trouble, unless you can spot the pitch down and away, like Greg Maddux or Tom Glavine. But that kind of control is rare.

You could talk to fifteen pitchers and get fifteen different opinions about pitching inside versus pitching down and away. Another pitcher might argue, "But, Randy, I don't have the same type of stuff that you've got, and I can't throw an 85-mph fastball inside without getting beat on that pitch."

I guarantee that if you throw an 85-mph fastball inside for effect, it will make your down-and-away change-up a lot more effective.

No matter how hard you throw the ball, or how much movement you put on the pitch, you still have to set up a hitter to get him out. And that means pitching inside—regardless of how hard you throw the fastball—to make him aware that he can't feel comfortable facing you.

These days, when you throw inside, a lot of hitters get upset and charge the mound, but in the 1950s and 1960s, pitching inside was a big part of the game. Bob Gibson and Don Drysdale pitched in to open up the middle/away zone of the plate. A hitter is not likely to dig in when getting hit with a 97-mph fastball crosses his mind, but the plan is never to hit the batter, because that's like handing him a free pass to first base.

Joe Kerrigan, a pitching coach in the Montreal Expos organization during my stint in the minors, taught me about body language and developing confidence in my pitches. In this sequence, I'm coming

to a high leg kick *(opposite)* as a checkpoint in my delivery and a key
to generating power, before breaking the ball from my glove *(above)*
as my weight is transferred in a forward direction.

I pitch inside more for immediate success, rather than to set up hitters for a down-and-away strike on the next pitch. But the goal is to keep the hitter off balance by avoiding patterns that are easy to recognize.

I throw three basic pitches: the four-seam power fastball, the two-seam sinking fastball, and the slider. I throw a slider down and in; a four-seam (95–97 mph) fastball or two-seam fastball down and in; and a 91–92-mph two-seam fastball down and away—which acts as my change-up.

Let's say I'm facing a right-handed hitter. I might start

No matter where I play baseball, I always want to give something back to the community.

him with a two-seam fastball down and away that'll be about 5 mph slower than my four-seamer. I've got him looking to the outside, and I'll bust a slider down and in, then maybe a four-seam fastball down and in. Now, if I get ahead in the count, I can come right back with a four-seam fastball away at 97 mph to strike him out because he was expecting the 92-mph two-seam fastball in that location. To the batter, they both look like the same pitch!

THE BIG BREAKTHROUGH

The one thing I want you to remember is that it is important to ask questions and seek out information from pitchers with more experience.

When I was called up to join the Expos in September 1987, I was part of a staff that included four quality veteran starters—Bryn Smith, Kevin Gross, Dennis Martinez, and Pascual Perez. But I went 3–0 with a 2.42 ERA in that month, and who is going to offer any advice to a young pitcher when things are going that well?

In 1989, I made the team out of spring training and got off to a terrible start in April (0–4, 6.67 ERA), found myself back in Indianapolis, and was promptly traded to Seattle. Practically overnight I was counted on as the ace of the staff.

As a result, I never had the chance to learn from an experienced starting pitcher. I didn't have anyone to tell me that I was dropping my shoulders and getting too emotional on the mound. Because I was so locked into the game, so intense about everything going on between the lines, I didn't even know that I was doing those things.

The nice thing about learning the ins and outs of pitching on my own is that I can share my experience with the young pitchers in Arizona. I enjoy teaching young pitchers how to learn from my experience. That's why I've gone on the Disney Channel to offer instructional tips, and it was one of my primary motivations in writing this book.

As I learned the hard way, not everyone has the luxury of pitching in a rotation with a veteran who can take you under his wing.

In 1992 in Seattle, I hit the wall with a run of eight consecutive losses. My mechanics were letting me down, and I decided to ask Nolan Ryan, who was pitching for the Texas Rangers at the time, for help.

Nolan and Tom House, a fellow USC Trojan and the Rangers pitching coach, analyzed my delivery during the 1992–93 period and detected a single but significant flaw that was causing all of my control problems: Every time I landed after releasing the pitch, my heel would spin off toward third base; all my weight would shift toward third, instead of heading in the direction of home plate; and my arm would drop down— all of which meant that my arm angle was inconsistent from one pitch to the next.

Nolan and Tom kept reminding me to fall on the ball of my foot—not on my heel—with my foot pointing toward home plate, not spinning over to third base.

This one major adjustment to my mechanics made all the difference in the world. It took me a long time to figure out what I'd been doing wrong all those years, but once I conquered this mistake, I began to master the other key elements of power pitching: mound presence, intimidation, and pitch selection and location.

It is not enough simply to be a good pitcher; you must

Working with kids and helping young athletes improve are among the things I enjoy most about playing baseball for a living.

make improvements at each stage of your development, or other pitchers will pass you along the way and you'll be left in the dust. The ability to improve is what distinguishes the pitchers who make it from the guys who don't quite have what it takes to go all the way to the top.

This book is about the things I believe in—mental intensity, precise mechanics, physical conditioning, intimidation, and a focus on winning. I hope it helps you progress and experience the rewards of hard work and 100-percent effort to fulfill your God-given potential.

MENTAL CONDITIONING FOR PITCHERS

The starting pitcher is at the center of the baseball universe. He is to baseball what the quarterback is to football. Everything revolves around what he does on the mound. He can make life either easier or harder for his teammates—and that is a great responsibility.

While pitching in Seattle, I had Ken Griffey Jr., Jay Buhner, and Edgar Martinez playing behind me and depending on me and my ability to give them a chance to win games. A team feeds off success. My mental intensity has rubbed off on my teammates in Seattle, Houston, and Arizona. And intensity begins with being mentally prepared to do the job I'm paid to do.

Young pitchers have the same responsibility to help out their teammates with a maximum effort. If you expect to be successful at any level, you have to put the time and hard work into preparing to pitch.

All athletes train physically in one way or another, but how many of them prepare mentally for the challenge at hand? You need to be familiar with your own strengths and weaknesses as well as those of your opponent.

The people who want to take their skills one step beyond the norm are the ones who achieve great things—and that statement applies to all career paths, not just throwing a baseball for a living. Success requires a tremendous expenditure of time and effort, and that work must begin at an early age.

Start evaluating your performances early on in your baseball career. As I mentioned at the outset, playing this game begins with having fun. Then, once you recognize that you have talent, start taking an inquisitive approach to improving your skills. Ask questions. Do research on the opposing team. And utilize your intelligence and mental energy to improve your on-field performance.

My mental intensity has rubbed off on my teammates in Seattle, Houston, and Arizona. And intensity begins with being prepared. Young pitchers have the same responsibility to help out their teammates with a maximum effort. You have to put time and hard work into preparing to pitch if you expect to be successful at any level.

R.J.'S TECHNIQUES FOR MAXIMUM MENTAL PERFORMANCE

Visualization Drill 1

To help improve my focus, I will visualize what I want to achieve in a particular game situation. I will isolate a visual zone—it could be a door on the other side of the room from where I'm standing—and then pick a smaller target, such as the doorknob, to focus my vision and block out everything else in the room.

Isolating the strike zone is based on the same principle. The zone has four corners. Don't focus on the middle of the zone as your primary visual target, since that's where you are most likely to get hurt by the hitter. It's easy to make the mistake of trying too hard to throw the ball over the plate for a strike and then hitting the middle of the strike zone (where you are likely to get beat) instead of hitting one of the four areas that surround the plate: up and in, out and in, down and in, down and away.

The ability to focus on those four areas—to pinpoint a minute section of the strike zone—was taught to me in the minor leagues.

I used to hear about trying to hit the catcher's shin-guards with a pitch to fine-tune my control. Visualization will improve your ability to focus and throw strikes.

Visualization Drill 2

Let's say I ask you to step back sixty feet and throw a baseball at a door. If your only goal is to hit the door with the baseball, your vision will take in the entire wall that surrounds the door. But if I ask you to throw the ball at a tiny spot on the door— the doorknob in the previous example, for instance—you are compelled to focus on that one visual zone instead of allowing your eyes to be distracted by the big picture.

I'm known for my ability to focus. And that does not just mean that I'm concentrating 100 percent of my mental energy on my objective of retiring the batter. I'm also thinking about hitting a particular zone of the plate to exploit his weakness. I will throw pitches down and in or down and away to take advantage of being ahead in the count.

Now let's say I'm ahead in the count. The hitter will be more likely to chase a high fastball because he can't afford to be selective. I'm not going to throw a ball right over the middle; instead, I'll pitch up and in or up and away.

If you're able to hit the glove as your ultimate target, with practice you'll be able to focus on one small section of the glove to further refine your control and the ability to spot your pitches in precise locations.

Visualization Drill 3

I will also visualize how I want to throw the pitch. I can form a mental image of the ball coming out of my hand; see it hit the precise zone where I want it to land; see the rotation on my slider as it leaves my hand; and see where the ball will cross the plate and where it will finish. To a left-handed hitter, the ball will appear way inside and then break over the inside corner; to a right-handed hitter, it will look as though it's outside, and then it will snap and catch the outside corner, or it can start over the middle and break down and in.

Visualization Drill 4

I will scan a lineup before the game, and visualize how I'll pitch to each hitter. After the first inning I have an even better idea of what I'm doing that day, and so I can visualize the next three hitters coming up in the second inning and develop a reasonably accurate appraisal of where I will throw my pitches.

As the game progresses, I have my pitching coach chart all the pitches I've thrown to a particular batter, and note what he did with those pitches. This prevents me from getting into a pattern of making the same mistake twice in a game.

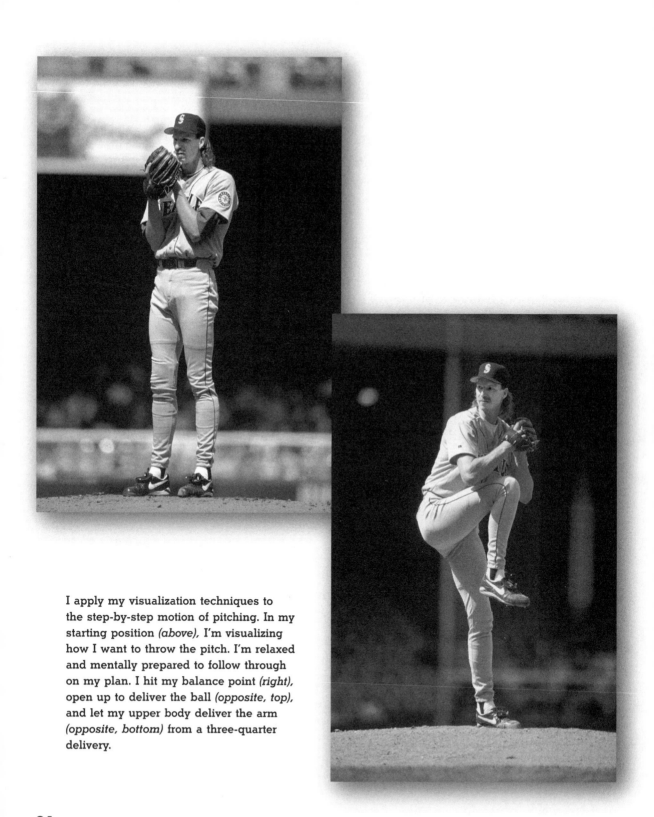

I apply my visualization techniques to the step-by-step motion of pitching. In my starting position *(above),* I'm visualizing how I want to throw the pitch. I'm relaxed and mentally prepared to follow through on my plan. I hit my balance point *(right),* open up to deliver the ball *(opposite, top),* and let my upper body deliver the arm *(opposite, bottom)* from a three-quarter delivery.

Now I release the pitch to the precise zone where I'd visualized it landing from the very beginning. I see the rotation on my slider as it leaves my hand. I can visualize where the ball crosses the plate and where it finishes—to a left-handed hitter, the ball will appear way inside and then break over the inside corner; to a right-handed hitter it will look as though it's outside and then snap and catch the outside corner, or it can start over the middle and break down and in.

When a hitter is coming up for the third or fourth at-bat, I may still throw him the same pitch, but I'll vary the location. He may be thinking that he saw a fastball on the first pitch twice in a row, and that's when he'll start looking for a fastball in that spot. The guy on deck will see that pattern as well, and he'll also be expecting that first-pitch fastball. I may still throw him the fastball, but you can bet it won't be in the same place.

Even though you may not have the luxury of a pitching coach to keep charts to track every pitch you throw, it is still within your power to take notes mentally on pitch selection to each batter during one of your games. You have only yourself to blame if you repeat history by throwing a high fastball to the same guy who hit a home run off a high fastball two innings before.

PITCHING AHEAD AND BEHIND IN THE COUNT

One of the most foolish ideas in baseball is that you should "waste" a pitch on an 0–2 count. You have the hitter where you want him. It is your job to put him away. I'm a strikeout pitcher, and I'm going to take care of business. Why mess around?

Your goal is to throw as few pitches as possible to dispose of that hitter. I want to get the batter out with the first pitch. That won't happen every time, of course, but the plan is to send the guy back to the dugout in three pitches or less.

Every pitch you throw in a particular sequence must have its own intrinsic value and meaning. If it does not retire the batter on its own, it should at the very least set up the next pitch that you are going to try to get him out with.

If I'm facing a right-handed batter, I'll throw a four-seam

fastball down and away. Let's say that it's a strike. I should know what the plan is on the next pitch now that I'm up 0–1 in the count. Now he's looking for an outside pitch, and instead I'll throw a slider down and in, or a fastball down and in.

Throw each pitch with a purpose. Don't waste pitches when ahead in the count on the pretext that you're saving energy for the later innings. Who is to say you'll still be around in the late innings?

That's why every pitch I throw, from the first to the last, is at maximum effort; I don't know when I'm going to be out of the game. Forget about pacing yourself. Pacing yourself for what?

I don't like goofing around. The fewer pitches it requires to get the guy out, the stronger I'll be if I'm fortunate enough to be pitching later in the game.

My ultimate goal is to get a weak groundball or flyball and end the at-bat straight away. Many hitters go up against me just trying to make contact and put the ball in play. This aggressive approach leads to peppering the ball foul until they finally get a pitch to drive—the pitch in a certain zone they are looking for.

Now it becomes an out-and-out chess match. If I have to exert more energy and throw multiple pitches to that batter, it's time to consider my options:

If I didn't get him out during the first two pitches, what happened? Did those pitches speed up his bat? That means I'll throw an off-speed pitch (my slider) because I can counter his bat speed with a slower pitch.

If I started him off with fastballs and sliders on the inside part of the plate, now he's consciously looking for an inside pitch, and I'll counter with a four-seam fastball on the outside part of the plate to catch him off guard.

Start evaluating your performances early in your baseball career. Start taking an inquisitive approach to improving your skills. Ask questions. Do research on the opposing team. And utilize your intelligence and mental energy to improve your on-field performance.

In a 2–0 or 3–0 count, you are playing to a hitter's strengths by being forced to come in with a strike. But when I fall behind, I'm not looking to throw a ball right over the heart of the plate—though that is what your natural instincts are telling you to do—because the hitter is looking to drive the pitch.

My goal is to hit my spots and to prevent the hitter from extending his arms—down and out, down and in, up and in are all viable locations.

A power pitcher has the luxury of being able to throw the ball right down the middle and often getting away with it because of superior velocity. Control pitchers like Greg Maddux and Tom Glavine of the Atlanta Braves, and Jamie Moyer of Seattle, must always have a set plan for each at-bat, each pitch, to set up the hitter, because if they get a pitch out over the plate, they're in trouble.

If you are a Greg Maddux type of pitcher, you'll have to use location as your method of getting the hitter out. I'm focusing on both velocity and location, which means I have two weapons at my disposal.

I know that with my velocity I'm manipulating bat speed—either I'll slow up the bat with the slider and then come in with the 98-mph fastball as the clincher, or I'll speed up the bat by showing the fastball and then fooling them with the slider.

Throwing strikes is 100 percent connected to success. Tom Glavine often struggles in the first inning of a ballgame because he likes to throw his change-up down and away, and some umpires won't call that pitch a strike. He's feeling his way through that inning to get a read on the strike zone for the outer part of the plate. The objective is to get ahead in the count with down-and-away fastballs and then induce a ground-ball out once the hitter is in a 1–2 hole.

Maddux and Glavine had to make adjustments in the 2001 season because the umpires refused to call the down-and-away pitch a strike—even though it was the same pitch in the same location that had been called a strike for years.

Suddenly Maddux and Glavine were forced to pitch more inside, and throw strikes instead of balls on the inside part of the plate.

A power pitcher doesn't have to worry so much about getting a called strike on the outer or inner part of the plate. I can immediately establish my dominance, throw strikes with my fastball or slider, and go about the business of controlling the flow of the game.

I don't have the pinpoint control of a Greg Maddux when he's trying to throw the down-and-away strike, but I can get away with throwing certain pitches over the plate.

My objective is to integrate the pitching-is-a-chess-match mentality of a Greg Maddux with the power and intimidation of a Nolan Ryan. I've tried to match location with velocity to take my game to another level.

I love watching Greg Maddux use his intelligence to

outsmart hitters. Outsmarting hitters is even more gratifying than blowing guys away with a fastball.

I remember striking out Todd Helton and Jose Ortiz of the Colorado Rockies to close out a game last year. They both took called third strikes because they were completely fooled; they were looking for sliders and I got them with fastballs.

Helton, one of the best hitters in baseball, never took the bat off his shoulder. The count was 0–2, and I have a tendency to throw my breaking ball when I'm ahead in the count.

This "pattern" of throwing sliders when I'm ahead works to my advantage in two ways: the hitter comes to expect it and I fool him with the fastball (like Helton and Ortiz), or I shake off my catcher, Damian Miller; the hitter might think I'm shaking off the slider for the fastball or the other way around. Now he has no clue what he's going to see.

You'll often see the hitter step out of the box in this situation because now I've got him thinking, *What the heck is R.J. doing?*

Turning pitching into a mental process is another step in your development as a pitcher. If I'm not content just to throw the ball by a hitter, then there's no reason why you can't push yourself to think on the mound about what pitch will work for you in any given situation.

If I establish that I'll throw my slider for a strike early in the count at the beginning of the game, then later in the game I can throw the slider out of the strike zone. The hitter will be forced to swing at the slider anyway, knowing that I was throwing strikes with it during the previous at-bat, because he doesn't want to fall behind in the count.

It works both ways, really, because if I don't demonstrate that I can throw the slider for a strike, why should he swing at that pitch? Any intelligent hitter will take the slider for a ball and wait on the fastball.

THE ART OF DECEPTION

I'm at my best when I can throw both the slider and the fastball for strikes. I will put even more on my pitches when everything is clicking. I can throw a backdoor slider—a sharp-breaking slider that moves from behind a lefty hitter to the inside corner, or from the outer part of the plate to a righty to nip the outside corner. The hitter will usually take this pitch for a strike, and now he's done me a favor.

One of the greatest feelings you will ever get as a pitcher is setting up a hitter and completely outsmarting him with a pitch he never expected to see in a million years.

To further deceive and confuse the hitter, some pitchers will hide the ball behind the glove until the very last instant before releasing it. Deception is to your advantage, because hitters need to be able to see the ball as soon as they can, to get a sense of where the pitch is coming from.

Hiding the ball behind your back or behind your glove until you get the ball out in front of the body is one way to throw off a hitter's timing. It's not something I've factored into my repertoire, but that doesn't mean it isn't worth considering if you are struggling or just looking for an extra advantage.

Trust me—everyone is a pitching coach when things are going wrong. One of the pitchers on the Colorado Rockies, a veteran who has enjoyed much success as a starter and as a reliever, has struggled through the 2002 season. That's the mental part of the game. He has the same ability that made him an All-Star and a twenty-game winner. It has been said that he doesn't have the same mound presence—an attitude, a stare, a sense of purpose—he once did when he was pitching well.

If the hitters are saying that about you—that you've lost the mound presence that tells the hitter you are confident or even intimidating—you had better go back to the drawing board to change your posture and mannerisms to exude confidence. Of course, this is easier said than done. When you continue to fail, it gets increasingly difficult to put positive information back in your head. That's why you need to work hard on the mental aspects of the game.

Your mind is strong enough to push you past the point of fatigue when your body is telling you to quit. I've had extra-inning games when my body wanted to shut it down, but my mind kept me going strong for another inning.

I can remember walking off the mound after the seventh inning of game five of the NLCS against the Atlanta Braves in 2001, when we were leading 3–2. I'd given up a run in the seventh, and they were beginning to put some hits together against me. Once I got out of that stressful situation, I had left everything I had—mentally and physically—out on the field.

Once your mind shuts down, there's no coming back. You can't turn it on and off like a light switch. That's how influential the mind is in determining what you can do—good or bad—as a pitcher.

A CLINIC ON MECHANICS

*M*echanics must be as simple as possible. More body movement means more chance for error. Efficiency and compactness are favored over flopping around all over the place.

The ideal delivery should follow from these basic steps:

1.   Stand upright with the balls of both feet on the rubber, the ball hidden within the glove, and your eyes on the catcher's target.

2.   Begin with windup by lifting your hands and coming to your balance point—your body in a tall, upright position with perfect posture. Once again, you are balancing on the balls of the feet—not shifting the weight to your heels.

3.   Make sure your hands break from the glove the same way every time you pitch.

4.   Begin to step or fall in a controlled and compact movement toward home plate with the front of your body: glove, knee, hip, shoulder, and elbow targeted squarely at home plate.

5.   Explode in a forward direction; remember that you can't generate any velocity until the ball is out in front of your body.

6.   The landing leg makes contact with the ground— you land on the ball of the foot, which is pointing at home plate.

7.   Now release the pitch from the ideal arm slot— elbows at shoulder height—to your target with 100 percent of your movement in a forward direction.

1. Stand upright in a tall position. Initiate the delivery by lifting your
hands and coming to your balance point.

2. Make sure your hand breaks from the glove the same way
every time you pitch.

3. Begin to step or fall in a controlled and compact movement
toward home plate.

4. Explode in a forward direction; remember that you can't generate any velocity until the baseball is out in front of the body.

5. Release the pitch from the ideal arm slot—
elbow is at shoulder height.

6. Follow through to your target with 100 percent of your movement in a forward direction.

I'm six feet ten, and I need to keep extraneous movement to an absolute minimum. Less movement is better because it leaves less room for error.

My balance over the mound is critical, because if I'm leaning off to one side or the other, by the time I release the ball the pitch could be off target. Balance is equally important at the end of the delivery because when I fall, I have to land on the ball of my foot.

BALANCE AND PRECISION

When I'm over the rubber, getting ready to throw the pitch, I want my weight on the ball of my foot or the instep (the arched middle part of the foot). I do not want the weight on my heel, because then I'll be leaning backward, which will force me to fall back and cause my arm to drop down so I won't be able to get my arm up on top in the correct position to deliver the pitch to home plate.

The most important lesson I learned in my entire pitching career was to start and end the delivery by balancing my weight on the ball of the foot. It is basic: You stand on the rubber on the ball of the foot at the outset of the pitching motion, and complete the delivery of the pitch by landing on the ball of the foot.

If you are putting your weight on your heel, over the rubber, you will fall backward, and if you land on your heel— what I was doing through most of my career before I met up with Nolan Ryan and Tom House in 1992—you will fall off toward third base and spin out of control.

THE STRATEGIC PLAN

The goal is to get your body to fall directly toward home plate and behind the full force of the pitch. It sounds easy, but it took me years to get this right.

When you place your weight on the ball of the foot over the rubber, you are standing tall.

As your momentum propels you toward home plate and you land (or fall) on the ball of your foot, you will be falling over the knee, which will be in a proper position, with a release point that's consistent, and with your body moving in a forward direction.

When I was landing (or falling) on my heel, my arm would drop down and my body would shift toward third base, and so my release point was doomed to be inconsistent from one pitch to the next.

There is no single correct way to pitch. All pitchers have different mechanics. And it is certainly possible to throw with unorthodox mechanics and still be successful. I'm living proof that you can have a basic flaw in your mechanics and still be overpowering.

Consistency is the key to being an effective pitcher. If you are having success with improper mechanics, some coaches will try to make corrections to put you on the right track. But who is to say that what you're doing is wrong, if it's working for you?

But you want to be consistent with your release point on every pitch. When I had improper mechanics, I wasn't consistent from one pitch to the next, and this hurt my ability to throw strikes.

It is just as important to be consistent with the position of your landing leg. If I land in the same spot every time,

I know that I'm throwing strikes and being efficient with my pitches.

When I was younger, I was landing all over the place—there were holes in the dirt all over the mound—and that made me inconsistent with my release point, because my arm would have to drag to catch up with where my body was going.

It is common sense that being inconsistent with where you land will also make you inconsistent with where you release the ball.

Any delivery is acceptable if you can apply the principles of proper mechanics to your pitching motion. A sidearm delivery is fine as long as you are consistent with the release point and each step of the process of throwing the pitch is repeated the same way every time.

I've never pitched sidearm or underhanded, though I have dropped down lower than my normal three-quarter delivery because of poor mechanics. With my height, the standard three-quarter delivery can be intimidating because it appears to the batter that I'm releasing the pitch very close to home plate.

I believe the three-quarter style makes me even more intimidating than releasing the pitch from over the top, because I'm a six-foot-ten left-hander with long arms and legs. So it looks to the batter as if the pitch is coming from second base, and it can be hard for him to see the ball coming out of my hand.

MECHANICS AND VELOCITY

I'm frequently asked how I'm able to throw with such velocity for an entire ballgame, often throwing harder in the sixth inning than in the first. With the application of precise mechanics, a starting pitcher can increase the velocity of his fastball and maintain that velocity throughout the game.

When I was falling off toward third base, my arm strength would decline as the game progressed, greatly decreasing my velocity in the later innings because I was putting too much stress on my shoulder.

As my mechanics improved, I became aware that velocity increases once you can put the strength of your entire body— not just your arm—behind the pitch. Now I had the power of 230 pounds behind my pitch, instead of relying only on my arm to generate velocity.

Summation of forces is a biomechanical principle that means the whole body is a single integrated unit moving toward a defined target. That's the goal of proper mechanics in a nutshell.

Through proper mechanics, arm strength can be increased as you get older. I'm thirty-eight years old and I can still hit 100 mph on the radar gun after throwing more than 125 pitches.

As a power pitcher, it is not unusual for me to throw harder at the end of the game than at the beginning, because I get into a groove. That may sound strange, because many pitchers tire as the game goes along, but there's no secret to my success other than hard work. And developing proper mechanics depends on making a commitment to repeating the same delivery, the same release point, the correct bio-mechanics, over and over again until it is second nature.

PITCH-COUNTS APPRAISED

A young pitcher's throwing program needs to be monitored, because you don't want to overload the elbows and shoulders with too many innings. The next thing you know, these kids are getting inflammations in the joints and are unable to develop their skills.

Major-league pitchers are monitored for the same reason. The goal of pitch-counts is to prevent arm injuries. In my particular situation, the game will dictate how many pitches I need to throw.

I remember the last time I ever pitched against Nolan Ryan. It was a hot afternoon in Arlington, Texas, while he was pitching for the Rangers and I was pitching for Seattle. This was the first time I'd hooked up with him after we met to go over my mechanics before the 1993 season. Nolan left the game with the score tied 2–2. I went on to throw 164 pitches over eight innings while recording eighteen strikeouts.

Throwing all those pitches will have an impact on the next few starts, and that was something I had to consider for the rest of that month. It is also true that if you throw a ton of pitches—say, thirty-five to forty-five—in one inning, it will carry over to the rest of that game. An arm is not designed to throw that many pitches in one inning. It is normal to throw fifteen to twenty-five pitches per inning, and beyond that it will take its toll on your elbow and shoulder.

Over the past three or four years, I've thrown more pitches than any other pitcher in baseball. That's not a stat I'm proud of, but I've had a lot of success during that span, and my ability to hold up under the strain of all those innings is a function of proper mechanics and conditioning.

I know that throwing so many pitches also comes with being a power pitcher who often leads the league in strikeouts. In some ways I'm a victim of my own success.

People often ask me if I enjoy striking guys out. The plain truth is that I'd rather still be pitching at the end of the game than sitting on the bench because I hit my pitch-count for that night in only six innings. To save my arm and keep me in the game for the long haul, I'd rather induce easy groundballs than strike out every guy on the other team.

NOTES ON LONGEVITY

Hard work has been the single biggest factor in my pitching effectively over such a long time. Of course, I've been blessed by God with a gift—and fine-tuning my mechanics helped me get the most out of that gift.

The other factor, quite honestly, is just having the desire to take my talent to another level. In the 2001 season, I came within eleven strikeouts of breaking Nolan Ryan's single-season record of 383. I had 372 strikeouts in 249.2 innings. Nolan set the record in 326 innings.

The funny thing was that no one ever mentioned I was closing in on the record with far fewer innings pitched than Nolan. During the 2001 season, I set a record for the highest strikeout-to-inning ratio (13.2 per nine innings) in major-league baseball history, and I'm proud of that accomplishment.

I didn't break the single-season record, though I came very close, because I skipped my final start to prepare for post-season play. The opportunity to play for a World Series ring meant more to me than setting an individual record—even a special one that's held by the man who had made a huge impact on my career.

PROPER PITCH POWER

Mechanics can make or break you, but improving the quality of your pitches is an essential element of enjoying success at any level of competition.

I rely on three pitches: the two-seam fastball, the four-seam fastball, and the slider. As I mentioned in chapter 1, I first learned how to throw a breaking ball when I was eleven or twelve years old. There's no predetermined rule for how old you need to be before you can throw a breaking ball. But I believe you should establish the success of your fastball before you start fooling around with off-speed pitches.

THE FASTBALL CLINIC

You can choose from two different fastballs: the two-seam (sinking) fastball and the four-seam (power) fastball.

Many young pitchers are unaware that the seams are placed on the baseball for a definite purpose. Never grip a fastball—two-seam or four-seam—on the slick part of the baseball. Pull with your fingers to produce backspin; in fact, the whole point of the seams is to get a better spin on the baseball.

A two-seam fastball is ideal for getting groundballs and throwing off the timing of the hitter. My two-seamer hits 92–93 mph, which is about 3–5 mph slower than my four-seamer. Changing speeds is one of many ways to confuse the hitter and keep him guessing.

Younger pitchers may want to begin with the four-seam fastball. If your hands are too small to throw this pitch with two fingers, then go with three fingers for now. Pull across the seams to create backspin, but remember the emphasis is still on throwing strikes—regardless of the pitch.

Two-Seam Fastball

My fingers are resting on and touching the two laces (or seams). Since I'm a left-handed pitcher, the ball will get a natural movement (or spin) to the left side of the plate. If you're a right-handed pitcher, the ball will get a natural movement to the right side of the plate. The faster the two-seamer spins, the more movement on the pitch and the more the pitch will sink.

Four-Seam Fastball

I grip this pitch across the four seams, and when the ball releases from my hand, the four seams rotate. On a four-seam fastball, the faster the ball spins, the more power that's generated on the pitch.

Slider

My fingers are slightly off to the side of the seams, but set together where a two-seam fastball would be gripped, and I'm looking to get a lot of wrist action coming out of my middle finger—which is the last finger that's going to push the ball out of my hand and make it rotate.

Ideal Arm Angle

Consistency is essential in your delivery. You can't vary your arm angle, or it will tip off the batter that you're throwing a particular pitch. I throw all my pitches from a three-quarter delivery to maximize power and intimidation—the release point will appear closer to the hitter as I follow through to deliver the pitch.

THROWING THE BREAKING BALL

I've always favored a slider over a curveball because it fits my power profile: a slider has a smaller, sharper break; a curveball has a bigger, slower break.

Nolan Ryan favored a curveball as his breaking ball of choice. Here's how he describes it:

> *"I grip the ball with the middle finger along the seam, and the index finger close by it. The downward wrist-snap drives the force across the ball. And the more seams that spin in the direction of the pitch, the greater the resistance placed on the rotation and the more the pitch will curve."*

The success of throwing the slider depends on the accuracy and precision of your mechanics. You have to experiment to see where the pitch will break, and you won't learn a thing if the ball is in the dirt all the time. Select a location from which to start the pitch and then check out where it's heading after it breaks.

Once again, the delivery of a slider should look exactly the same as the delivery of a fastball. The hitter is not going to know it's a slider until the pitch breaks at the last instant, but at that point it's too late for him to adjust.

5

PHYSICAL CONDITIONING FOR PITCHERS

I believe in taking a critical approach to devising a workout program: Are you doing exercises that are functional? Are you building up the muscles that simulate swinging a bat or throwing a baseball? I learned how to apply sport-specific, functional training—defined simply as exercises that train the muscles you use in performing your physical activity—to my routine in 1996 after I injured my spine, and it has been a huge benefit to my performance and in extending the length of my career.

I've learned the importance of having good balance over the rubber, which means my arm won't drag on the follow-through, and being consistent with the correct mechanics to establish consistency and efficiency.

After my back surgery in 1996, my physician told me I was getting 50 percent of my velocity from my core—spine, lower back, and abdominals. I never knew that before my injury. I'd never done any specific exercises to increase the strength of my lower back, glutes, and hamstrings. Those are the muscle groups that take a pounding when you are pitching.

Strengthening those key target zones with stabilizing exercises makes my core stronger over the mound and lets my body deal with the torque and exertion on my abs and spine. All that torque led to my back problems, and the functional training routine I advise for pitchers is the best way to prevent such overuse injuries and keep you pitching healthy for years to come.

THE ORIGIN OF THE PROGRAM

My training regimen took shape after the 1995 season with the Seattle Mariners, in which I went 18–2 with a 2.48 ERA. I beat the New York Yankees twice in the NLDS, and pitched well against Cleveland in the NLCS. I went to spring training in '96 with tremendous optimism. The team was very upbeat after a taste of success, which quieted the rumors about the Seattle Mariners relocating to Tampa.

Unfortunately, I was having all sorts of back problems that spring. When the Mariners got to Anaheim to play the Angels, I went to see a back specialist after an MRI revealed that I had a bulging disk in my lower back. He put me on a program to strengthen my lower back to reduce the pressure on the disk.

I went through the prescribed exercise program, and though it helped me deal with the pain, it was not going to solve the problem caused by the wear and tear of throwing a baseball 98 mph on a six-foot-ten-inch frame. I was unable to pitch with perfect mechanics because of the constant pressure on my lower back, and obviously that affected my ability to be effective.

I tried to pitch through the pain, but it finally reached the point of no return in September, when I flew down to Los Angeles to have back surgery performed by Dr. Robert Watkins at Centinela Hospital—one of the most highly respected sports medicine centers in the United States.

The plan was to get the back operation on September 12, not pick up anything heavier than a coffee cup for about a month, and then spend the off-season doing rehab in Phoenix—where I was living at the time—to prepare for the 1997 season.

The Mariners' spring training base was in Peoria, and I was living with my family in Glendale—about a ten-minute commute to the rehab center—so it all worked out quite nicely.

The road back from the surgery was gradual and incremental. I took small steps at the outset to get the movement and flexibility to return. It was a five-month rehab process, with five to six days a week of physical therapy. The longer I got into doing it, the stronger I became and the longer the exercise sessions would last.

The end product of this five-month physical conditioning regimen was a stronger core—abs, lower back, and hamstrings, with added flexibility. I was rewarded with a greater awareness of how my body worked as a multi-link chain in the process of delivering a baseball through proper mechanics.

Many of the physical therapy exercises were functional movements to simulate the biomechanics of pitching: bending over; strengthening the muscles that I used as a pitcher. In performing those exercises I was able to realize that as good as I had been up until that point, I could now take my game to another level. I was mixing in sport-specific conditioning to prevent my body from breaking down—and this would become increasingly important as I got older.

The exercises I learned from Brett Fischer, my physical therapist during my rehab, became the basis of my standard workout routine. Brett's emphasis on designing an exercise program that simulates the sport or activity that you perform on a regular basis was way ahead of its time.

The exercises that you see in the photos were virtually unknown in 1996, but today they form the basis for the workout routines of many of the pitchers on the Arizona Diamondbacks and other big-league clubs.

The large therapy ball—an obscure workout tool when I did my rehab—is now a fixture in exercise programs, gyms, and physical therapy centers all over the United States.

When you first look at me working with the ball, it doesn't appear to have anything to do with throwing a baseball. But I enjoyed the benefits on a firsthand basis because it helped me right away, both as a rehab tool and as a way to continually improve my strength, balance, and flexibility.

Fitness is extremely important for a pitcher. Shoulder exercises (especially ones that train the rear deltoids, at the back of the shoulder) with dumbbells are part and parcel of a pitcher's workout regimen. The rear delts take the brunt of the force of a pitch as they slow down your arm when it follows through to deliver the ball.

Dr. Frank Jobe, a widely respected orthopedic specialist, is often associated with the "Jobe dumbbell exercises," which are designed to strengthen the rotator cuff. All pitchers need to recover from their previous performance and be prepared physically for peak results in the next performance.

To reach those goals, you must to get the lactic acid out of your shoulder, and build the muscles back up that you've torn down in your previous start.

Any baseball coach or trainer can show you how to implement the Jobe dumbbell exercises. You can refer to *Nolan Ryan's Pitcher's Bible* (Simon & Schuster, 1991) for photos and detailed explanations. But young pitchers should work in concert with the coaching staff at their school to design a program that is right for them.

Strong legs are important, more to some pitchers than others. Drop-and-drive pitchers like Tom Seaver and Roger Clemens put top priority on doing leg exercises. I pitch with all of my upper body. I'm a tall pitcher, and I get a lot of leverage from my top half; in fact, most of my velocity is generated by the torque that I put on my spine.

I will train my legs, but I place more emphasis on shoulders, rotator cuff, and posterior delts in particular, as well

The pitching motion puts a tremendous amount of stress on the body, especially the muscles at the back of the shoulder (the rear deltoids) that slow down the arm as it follows through to deliver the pitch. I've learned the importance of having good balance over the rubber, which means my arm won't drag on the follow-through, and being consistent with the correct mechanics to establish consistency and efficiency. Fitness for a pitcher is extremely important. Shoulder exercises (especially ones that train the rear delts) with dumbbells

are part and parcel of a pitcher's workout. And strengthening the key target areas—
lower back, glutes, hamstrings, and abdominals—with stabilizing exercises makes my core
stronger over the mound *(opposite)* and lets my body deal with the torque and exertion
(above) on the abs and spine. All that torque led to my back problems, and the functional
training routine I advise for pitchers is the best way to prevent those overuse injuries and
to keep you pitching healthy for years to come.

as abdominals, lower back, and hamstrings (the three areas that I refer to as my core). I need to keep those areas strong to maintain my velocity over the 100-plus pitches I throw in a typical start.

RANDY JOHNSON'S WORKOUT SCHEDULE

Day 1

Pitching day.

Day 2

The first day after a start, I will get a rubdown on my shoulders and lower back to accelerate the recovery process and to loosen everything up. I then go into the weight room to train my legs—no need to work on the upper body the day after pitching. I will do the basic leg exercises you'd find in any strength-building regimen—leg curls (hamstrings), leg extensions (thigh muscles), and calf raises—but your coach will tell you what to do in keeping with the objectives of your particular program.

LOWER BACK

I do an exercise called Around the World (see photos), in which I balance on one leg and use a ten-pound exercise ball to put all the resistance on the glutes and lower back.

I also perform at least two other exercises for lower back and abs (see photos and captions of "The Bridge" and "Stabilization Variation") that rely on the inflatable exercise ball.

At the end of the workout I'll do an interval program on the stationary bike to elevate my heart rate.

Day 3

UPPER BODY WEIGHT TRAINING AND LONG TOSS
I do an assortment of back, shoulder, bicep, and tricep exercises, and always include the Jobe dumbbell program to strengthen the rotator cuff.

THROWING ROUTINE
I play long toss with Damian Miller for ten minutes. We'll start about 100 feet apart and gradually increase the distance in ten-foot increments. The goal is to stretch my arm out after taking a two-day break from throwing the baseball.

Day 4

I throw on flat ground in a side session with a catcher. Nolan Ryan told me to do my throwing on flat ground instead of the elevated mound because it is less stressful on the arm. Throwing off the mound is a tearing-down process, and I don't really need to put my body through that on the third day after pitching. This routine is not for everybody, but it has worked well for me.

Jobe dumbbell program.

Day 5

Light cardio on the bike.

Jobe dumbbell program.

Physical Conditioning for Pitchers

This is a typical workout that I perform the day after pitching up until two days before one pitch.

Around the World

I begin with a 10-pound exercise ball and I'm balancing all my weight on my left foot and bending over. I start from the outside of my left foot and working my way around full circle (I will finish at the outside of the left foot) as I raise up and extend back down in increments of 1 or 2 feet—I'm setting the ball

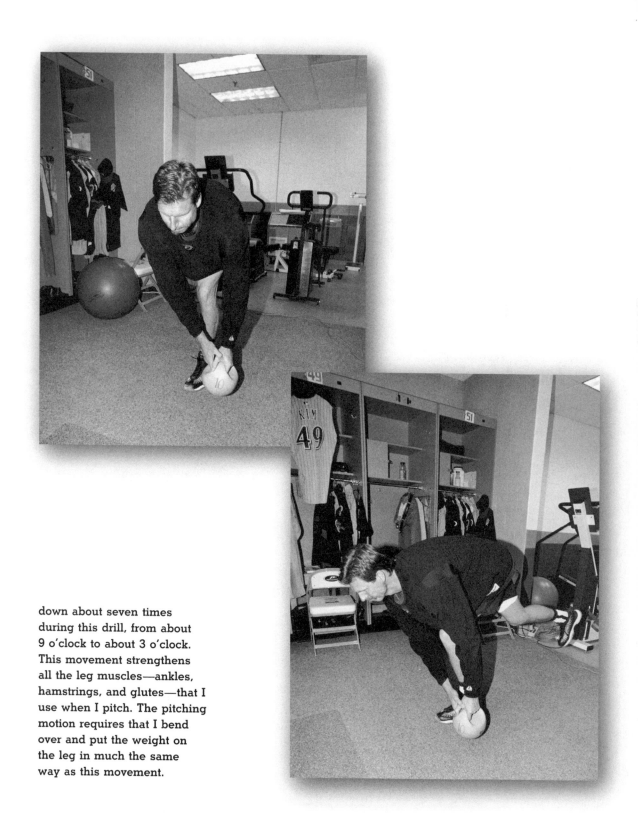

down about seven times during this drill, from about 9 o'clock to about 3 o'clock. This movement strengthens all the leg muscles—ankles, hamstrings, and glutes—that I use when I pitch. The pitching motion requires that I bend over and put the weight on the leg in much the same way as this movement.

Exercise 1: Stabilization Variation

I'm in a push-up position, arms shoulder-width apart, with my shins resting on an inflatable exercise ball. I'm rocking back and forth on the ball, and using the strength of my abdominal muscles to stabilize my body. This is a core exercise designed to stabilize and strengthen the abs and lower back. I'm also strengthening the shoulders as I rock back and forth on the ball.

Exercise 2: The Bridge

I'm arching my back on an exercise ball that's resting on my shoulder blades. I'm rocking back and forth while the back muscles fire to stabilize my body.

Day 6

It's time to make another start in the rotation. I'm physically prepared to take the ball, and I'm mentally prepared to pitch against my opponent. I've looked over the pitching charts to get a sense of what I've done to pitch successfully against them in the past, and of what I need to do to make mental adjustments and strategic adjustments for continued success.

Program Modifications

I get into a specific routine because it helps establish a pattern for what I need to do every day to prepare for my next start. But I will add and subtract training techniques to keep everything fresh and my mind open to new ideas.

During the 2001 season, for instance, I started using a small therapeutic pool, where you swim against a current, for low-resistance conditioning. And following every start, I take a Jacuzzi to target the water jets on my shoulders to get the blood flowing back into the muscles and to trigger the recovery process.

I have to modify my workout schedule toward the end of the baseball season to give my body a chance to heal and recover from the grind of pitching every fifth day; nevertheless, I still always do something to maintain my strength.

I've learned through trial and error that I can't train with the same volume of exercise in September, after making thirty-two starts, as I could in May, after my seventh start. I want to save my strength for my primary concern—pitching every fifth day to the best of my ability.

RANDY JOHNSON'S OFF-SEASON CONDITIONING PROGRAM

I take a one-month break from training to give my mind and body a chance to recover from the 162-game schedule.

Weight Training

My primary goal is to pack on some bulk and strength by lifting with heavier weights than I would during the baseball season, and to add compound lifts such as bench presses (which I stay away from during the season for fear of getting tight in the pectoral region) to enhance my overall symmetry and upper-body strength.

I lift weights four days per week with at least one intensive cardio session and some light cardio on my lifting days. I will cut back on the reps and increase the weight relative to the in-season routine.

Throwing

I start playing light catch out in my front yard after Christmas. I begin to play long toss from mid-January until early February. I start pitching off the mound in the two weeks leading up to reporting to spring training in Tucson on February 14.

A DAY
IN THE LIFE
OF A
POWER PITCHER

APRIL 11, 2002

ARIZONA DIAMONDBACKS VS. COLORADO ROCKIES AT COORS FIELD

This was one of those starts that will tell you a lot about what it's like to be a power pitcher, and about the ups and downs all pitchers go through—no matter how dominating they appear to the casual observer.

Power pitchers often struggle in the first inning. The plan is to get into a groove, establish dominance and take charge of the game right from the start. If there's even the slightest mechanical flaw, however, it is an uphill battle even to get ahead in the count.

As a power pitcher, I have to bring an aura of intimidation with me to the mound. Nolan Ryan would stare down hitters. Sandy Koufax would intimidate hitters with his stuff. The aura of a power pitcher is a mix of body language, a menacing stare, and the fear factor that goes with forcing hitters to cope with a 100-mph fastball.

Keep in mind that this was an early-in-the-season start. On opening day I threw 127 pitches in a complete-game shut-out. My next outing was in Milwaukee in very cold weather, and I threw 114 pitches. I had really extended myself in those first two starts, and developed some soreness and inflammation in my shoulder.

I skipped my usual side-throwing session between starts to let the shoulder recover, and that rusty feeling had an impact on this night in Colorado.

My shoulder felt stiff. I knew that I had terrible stuff when I was warming up in the bullpen. And I made the mistake of bringing that bad stuff out with me to the mound.

I took the mound on a cold, crisp night at Coors Field in the Rocky Mountains. It's a ballpark that's notorious for creating problems for pitchers. The thin air and high altitude allow the ball to carry farther than seems possible. On this night I felt vulnerable in the first inning. I did not have my best fastball or my good slider, so I had to put more effort into the chess match that goes with changing speeds, spotting my pitches, and outsmarting the hitter.

My usual approach to Juan Pierre—the Rockies lead-off hitter, who tends to give me trouble because he's very aggressive—is to pitch him inside. On this night, though, those pitches were missing too far inside because my shoulder was stiff and I was not yet into the flow of the game.

Before I could even break a sweat, the Rockies loaded the bases with two runs in, no outs. Now, a 2–0 lead is not going to hold up in Coors Field. I kept my mind focused on making good pitches, and I escaped without any more damage.

As I walked off the mound, I was thinking, *If I don't pitch any better than that, I'm going to put my team in a hole, so I'd better step it up a bit.*

❍   ❍   ❍

You have to put yourself in my shoes to understand a pitcher's mentality in this situation: The expectations coming into the game are always that I will dominate from the first out until the last—or until I give way to the bullpen after the seventh or eighth inning. Right from that first hitter, Juan Pierre, it is painfully clear that these "expectations" are not going to pan out. It is a new script, one that no one expected, and it is up to me to stay focused on damage control instead of raw power and intimidation.

Bob Brenly, the Arizona Diamondbacks manager, came up to me after the game and compared what had happened— and how I had handled it—to a game in 2001 against the St. Louis Cardinals. In the St. Louis game I was equally ineffective—bad mechanics and no overpowering fastball or slider. But in that game, on April 8, 2001, I let the situation get the better of me. I didn't try to pitch with what I had, or make the necessary adjustments to get guys out without having my best stuff. I continued to hit batters with pitches, and

If I'm out there struggling, it is hard to maintain that aura of intimidation that everyone in baseball associates with a typical Randy Johnson performance. A lot of people in the stands are asking, "Where are his fastball and nasty slider? Is he even trying?" I am as vulnerable as any pitcher if I don't have my best stuff. But the goal is not to let my body language— what I define as my mound presence—send a message to my teammates or the opposing team than I'm in trouble and struggling with my confidence.

People call me intimidating, and I enjoy hearing that kind of talk. If you're intimidated by me, I'm 50 percent of the way to beating you before you step up to the plate. In this particular game against the Rockies, I was suddenly "beatable" in the first inning. But that does not mean I'm going to make it easy on you and give in. I always project the mentality that I expect to win. I never consider the possibility of losing when I take the mound to start a game.

yielded back-to-back home runs to Eli Marrero and Mike Matheny. At the end of the night I had given up nine earned runs in five and two-thirds innings, and we'd lost 9–4.

This need to make adjustments applies to all pitchers. A guy who lives and dies with his change-up also depends on pinpoint location. If that location fails him during a start, he becomes vulnerable.

I am as vulnerable as any pitcher if I don't have my best stuff. But the goal is not to let my body language—what I call my mound presence—send a message to my teammates or the opposing team that I'm in trouble and struggling with my confidence.

That was Brenly's point in our post-game conversation. In the ballgame I pitched against the Cardinals, I didn't have my best stuff, I was feeling vulnerable, and I was communicating that to the hitters with my body language. I was dropping my shoulders and looking upset.

Body language is an important and very underrated element of pitching. Let's say one of your infielders commits an error that puts you in a jam. In the sixth inning of the game against Colorado, for instance, Junior Spivey (the Arizona second baseman) rushed his throw to first on a grounder by Todd Zeile, and Zeile was credited with a hit on the play, but it could have been scored an error.

But my body language did not show that I was upset. The goal is to support your teammates at all times. And later in the inning, Spivey made a dive onto the outfield grass to snare a hard liner—that's how fast you can redeem yourself in this game.

I pitch with a lot of emotion and a lot of adrenaline. Early in my career, I would have let my emotions take over, and my body language—dropping my shoulders—would have conveyed how I was feeling.

Your teammates are working as hard to win the game as you are, and it is not acceptable to show them up. I often ask my catcher, Damian Miller, to keep an eye on my mound presence when I'm not pitching up to par. On this night he reminded me not to let my early struggles distract me from focusing on getting my groove back.

Struggling in the first inning is an occupational hazard of a power pitcher. I'm trying to find my fastball, trying to get the feel of my slider. I'm trying to get comfortable with the "real" mound as opposed to the bullpen mound, and the tendency is to bring the problems of the warmup session into the game with me. And I'm working to figure out the strike zone of the umpire and get into the flow of the game very quickly.

In '99 with the Diamondbacks, there were several games where I gave up a run in the first inning and we lost the game either 1–0 or 2–1. One of the principal rules of pitching is never to give up a run after your team has scored a run, and you never want to give up a run in the first inning and put your team in a hole.

I will have trouble getting into the flow of the game until I establish my fastball and feel comfortable with my mechanics. This applies as well to Nolan Ryan and Roger Clemens—two other top power pitchers—who rely on the fastball to get ahead in the count and get into that groove that spells strikeouts and intimidation.

Larry Walker, one of the best hitters in baseball over the past ten years, and my teammate a long time ago in the Montreal Expos organization, went 1–3 with a double in the Colorado game. He understands what it is like to hit against me, and here is his take on my intimidation factor:

It's very intimidating, stepping up to the plate against R.J., knowing that he is a giant and his release point is going to appear to be only a few feet away from you—that's a big intimidation factor right there! But the primary goal when hitting against him (or any power pitcher) is to shorten up on the swing and let his power feed into my power.

The amazing thing about Randy is how he went from just being a raw thrower when I knew him in Montreal to being one of the best control pitchers in baseball history. With the Expos, his mechanics were so out of whack that he didn't have a clue where the pitch was headed.

After we found out about his trade from Montreal to Seattle, he and I were riding in a cab over to the ballpark, and I told him it had to be the stupidest trade in baseball history. [Editor's note: Randy was traded with pitchers Brian Holman and Gene Harris in exchange for pitchers Mark Langston and Mike Campbell.] In R.J. we're talking about a left-handed pitcher (a rare commodity, to say the least) who could throw 100 mph and scare people to death. All he needed was the right coaching to put it together, and he has become one of the best pitchers ever to play the game.

His slider is almost impossible to hit because it starts out of the middle of the plate and it eats you up on your hands after it breaks inside at the last minute.

But the most impressive thing about Randy is his intensity. He gets himself into every single start. He has so many ways of beating you—from throwing hard to hitting his spots to looking mean on the mound.

You can see clearly how my upper body helps me deliver the pitch *(above)*, and how my arm releases the pitch while the ball of my foot is landing on target toward home plate *(opposite)*. Knowing my mechanics and how to check for mistakes is a big help on nights when I struggle. In this game against

Colorado, my teammates never doubted I'd get it together. The numbers often speak for themselves. I have made a name for myself in Seattle, Houston, and Arizona. The expectation is that I will accept nothing less than success, and the focus on winning helps to make the players around me even better.

He has made enormous strides, and much of the credit has to go to hard work and his commitment to improving as his career has progressed.

People call me intimidating, and I enjoy hearing that kind of talk. If you are intimidated, that's fine with me; I'm 50 percent of the way to beating you before you step up to the plate.

Intimidation is not as much a conscious effort to scare a hitter as a side effect of intensity. After that bleak first inning in the Rockies game (two runs allowed, one hit, two walks, one hit batter), I settled down and only gave up one more hit over the next six innings, and we came back to win 8–4.

That intensity I bring to the mound has an impact on the other four starting pitchers in the Diamondbacks rotation. It is the same trickle-down effect that you see with the Atlanta Braves' Greg Maddux, Tom Glavine, and John Smoltz. It is a professional competition with the idea being, "I'll try to match what you did tonight because it was good enough to win the game."

I'm pleased that I'm able to have a major impact on other pitchers, because the message is to integrate mound presence, focus, mental preparation, and proper mechanics. This isn't a game that allows you to get away with a lack of preparation. You might get away without being prepared a few times, but inevitably that lazy approach will come back to haunt you.

In the game against the Rockies, I was suddenly "beatable" in the first inning. Yeah, I'm "beatable" in theory, but you'll have to bring your "A game" to bring me down. I always project the mentality that I expect to win. I never expect to lose when I take the mound to start a game.

Mark Connor, my pitching coach with the Diamondbacks in 1999 and 2000, understands my winner-take-everything attitude:

The thing you have to understand about Randy is that it kills him to lose a game. He would rather give up five earned runs and win 7–5 than lose a 1–0 game in which he had twenty strikeouts. In 1999, when Randy first arrived in Arizona, he lost four games in a row: 1–0, 2–0, 1–0, and 2–0. We were on the road in San Diego after that fourth consecutive loss, and he wanted to talk for a few minutes, just to clear his mind and to put everything in perspective. He said to me in all candor, "I don't understand what I'm doing wrong. What is it going to take to be able to win a game?"

I reminded him that he is not Superman. He can't be perfect every time—despite the fact that he strives for perfection, and that is also what the media expects of him. The point is that 99 percent of the pitchers in baseball would have been satisfied with how they pitched, and Randy was going out of his mind because the team was not winning games.

I was the Toronto Blue Jays pitching coach, and had the challenge of working with a very young pitching staff. I often wished that these young guys could have sat down and had lunch with Randy and picked his brain about pitching. I actually learned a lot from Randy from talking pitching, different situations and strategies, but the most valuable lesson was his refuse-to-lose mentality. A lot of people in this game believe that starting pitchers are selfish. Randy's only concern is giving his team a chance to win every time he takes the baseball to the mound, and that is why he is so special.

The Arizona Diamondbacks went from losing 100 games the year before Randy got here to winning the National League West in '99. And we did that without Curt Schilling. Randy had it all on his shoulders; the intensity that he brought with him to the mound helped show the rest of the team what it would take to win a championship.

I pride myself on winning, and yet I have learned more about the craft of pitching from losing games and surviving adversity than from pitching with constant success.

Nolan Ryan once told me, "You can't let the failure of your last pitch affect the success of your next pitch."

That common sense from Nolan applies to the first inning of the ballgame against the Rockies. I could not let what happened with the first three or four hitters influence how I pitched to the next three or four.

Here is what went down in the inning: I hit Juan Pierre with a pitch. Pierre stole second, and Juan Uribe tripled down the right-field line and Pierre scored (1–0 Colorado).

I walked Larry Walker and Todd Zeile. Tony Womack bobbled Todd Helton's grounder, Uribe scored (2–0 Colorado), and now I was in that bases-loaded, no-out situation we talked about earlier.

I could have made bad pitches because I was frustrated with the error, with my lack of control, or with my impatience at dealing with failure. But instead I sucked it up and got Benny Agbayani and Jose Ortiz to strike out swinging, and made Bennett hit a grounder to Mark Grace at first to end the inning.

I went through a stretch early in my career in Seattle where I lost eight starts in a row. I learned more from that period of failure than from winning eight games in a row, which I've done several times. I started putting more time into analyzing my mechanics, examining videotapes of games, asking questions, watching other pitchers, and seeking help from coaches and other players.

When the chips are down, you need mental toughness to overcome failure.

I relied on my mental powers in Colorado, and we went on to win and sweep the rest of the four-game set at Coors Field. After having no idea where my pitches were going in the first inning, I came back with strikeouts against Agbayani and Helton in the sixth and finished the night with a slider to jam Juan Pierre on the inside corner (for my ninth strikeout of the evening) and retire the side in the seventh.

To reach your full potential, you will need to develop mental toughness to complement your natural physical ability. This is not just an abstract concept. It simply means you don't let a game get out of hand when things start going wrong. You continue to focus on making good pitches with men on base. Show your teammates that you are supportive of them—even when they commit an error that puts you in a bind.

When the mental and physical talents mesh, only then will you have something special to build on.

7

THE PITCHER-CATCHER CONNECTION

I'm very lucky that I've had the opportunity to collaborate with Damian Miller, one of the most underrated catchers in baseball, during my four-year stint with the Arizona Diamondbacks. (Damian Miller was traded to the Chicago Cubs following the 2002 baseball season.)

Damian works with me on pitch selection. He understands my strengths and weaknesses, and those of the hitter. He knows—and a pitcher should be aware of these things as well—whether the hitter is cheating: moving up in the box, moving back in the box, moving off the plate, or moving closer to the plate.

I've told Damian on many occasions that his ability to help all five of our starters on the Diamondbacks maximize their ability every single day is more important to this club than how he performs with the bat, though he is a very good hitter.

He is dedicated to a thorough and meticulous pre-game preparation, going over the opposing lineup so that we have a specific strategic plan each night.

A good catcher is worth his weight in gold. Damian's ability to help me in several phases of pitching is a perfect example of how the pitcher-catcher dynamic should work to your advantage.

Damian will pick and choose when to come out to the mound to talk to pitchers to discuss strategy, pitch selection, or location. He will give me a breather when things are going bad. You don't want to let a jam snowball into a big inning for the other team. He will ask me to step off the mound and gather my thoughts. A veteran pitcher should be able to do that without any help from the catcher, but in some cases you might get so locked into the game that you don't even realize your ability to focus is slipping away.

Damian is very adept at calming me down. And he will talk to me between innings, providing a game plan for starting

Damian Miller is one of the best defensive catchers in baseball. He has an excellent throwing arm, and keeps me focused on throwing quality pitches with runners on base.

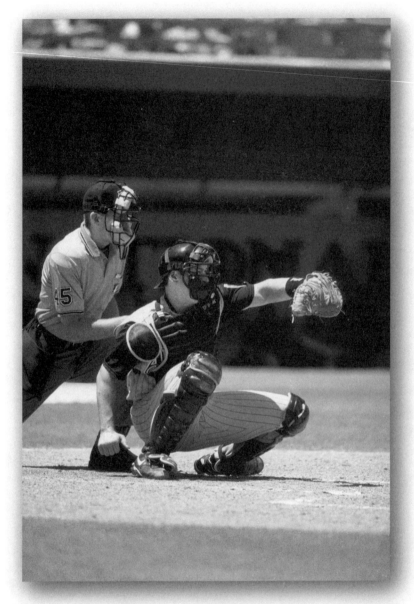

Damian and I go over the opposing team's lineup before each of my starts to analyze what they've done in the past against me. The way we pitch to Barry Bonds of the San Francisco Giants is a good example of how we deal with a dangerous hitter. Barry hit his first home run against me during the 2002 season, but I'm not afraid to pitch to him. You have to be a smart pitcher. If you fall behind in the count against a hitter like Bonds—or the best hitter on the opposing team—you don't want to throw him anything down the heart of the plate, because he can afford to be more selective. If you get ahead in the count, you still have to pitch carefully to him, but now you have the upper hand and can dictate what pitches you want to throw, and which location plays more to your strengths.

off a hitter based on what I've done in the past. At times I've shaken him off, and I've regretted it because his judgment on pitch selection is incomparable.

Damian plays to my strengths. If I have my good fastball and I'm facing Sammy Sosa, who is a good fastball hitter, I always want to get beat with my best pitch; in other words, I'm not going to back down. Damian knows that, and then it's just a matter of location: Where can I throw my best pitch to exploit a weakness Sosa may have with a particular hitting zone?

When I'm struggling—and the game we analyzed against the Colorado Rockies is an excellent example—Damian works with me to find my strength on that day. In the first inning of the April 11, 2002, game, I had no clue what my strength was, because nothing was working. He stayed with the slider until it finally came around, and my fastball fell into line later in the game, once I established that I could throw the slider for strikes.

He also had me fine-tune my location, as my pitches were not effective. We pitched inside instead of out over the middle of the plate. My shoulder was flying open, and that's why a lot of the strikes were down and in—not knee-high and in for strikes.

The bottom line is that my location was good, but I did not have my best fastball. I was challenging hitters, but I did not want to challenge them over the heart of the plate. Damian understood this, so we worked inside, we worked down and away, and he had me throw some split-finger fastballs to offset my fastball.

Damian will come into the clubhouse after batting practice, and we'll put together a game plan. Before the April 11 game against the Colorado Rockies, we went over the lineup to devise a strategy based on the past success or failure of the opposing team.

I had a good working relationship with my catcher in Seattle, Dan Wilson, as well as with my manager, Lou Piniella. Lou understood pitching, and I respect his baseball knowledge. Remember that catchers and coaches come out to the mound to calm you down and get you focused on making good pitches. Don't let the failure of your last pitch affect the success of your next pitch.

Juan Pierre has done well against me, so we decided to pitch him inside because he's a slap-hitter who will spray the ball the other way—to left, since he is a left-handed hitter—and utilize his speed. If I pitch him away, he'll drive the ball to left and try to hit it over the third baseman's head. In fact, on one of his at-bats he smoked a line drive right to third base—exactly what he was trying to do.

We decided to pitch him inside, but the problem was that I was coming in too far inside and struggling with my mechanics. I was throwing a lot of two-seam fastballs to him, and the one that hit him simply got away from me.

Larry Walker is another hitter on the Rockies who I want to pitch inside, and then down and away. I don't want to throw the ball out over the heart of the plate because I know he can drive that pitch and do damage.

With a hitter I can handle, such as Benny Agbayani, I just want to make it clear to Damian that if we get ahead with the fastball—and Benny is a dead fastball hitter—we should go to the breaking ball. I want to spot my fastball but then go to my strength, which is the slider, with the aggressive, free-swinging hitters who are looking for fastballs. The point is to exploit the weakness of the hitter with a pitch he is either not expecting or is unable to handle with any consistency.

That's why it is so important to head to the mound with a plan of action. You can't just go with your best stuff, play it by ear, and hope for the best. Major-league hitters are too good for that.

Here is what Damian has to say about our collaboration in Arizona:

Randy Johnson is the best pitcher in baseball when it comes to working out of trouble. He honestly believes that no one should ever get a hit off him. He's one of those rare pitchers who can gain an extra 3–4 mph on his fastball with men on base. Now we're talking about upgrading from a 95-mph fastball to a 98- or 99-mph fastball, and that ability to dig deeper and improve under pressure is what sets him apart from the rest of the pitchers in the game.

As a catcher, I must know about my pitchers and be able to appreciate how challenging it is to deal with smaller ballparks, stronger hitters, and a shrinking strike zone. Randy has completely dominated in the past five years, at a time when pitchers are clearly at a disadvantage. He is a power pitcher who has sensational control because he is a student of the game.

Young pitchers must learn to work off the fastball—the pitch that sets up your breaking ball— and be able to throw strikes on both sides of the plate. They must be able to maintain a consistent release point and arm angle, and fine-tune their mechanics. Randy had to struggle with all of these elements of pitching before he became great, and his example of hard work and dedication to success and winning is something we can all learn from.

When my career is over, I'll look back and realize that I had the chance to collaborate with a first-ballot Hall of Fame pitcher who put 100 percent of his mental and physical energy into every start he made.

In my book he's the most dominating left-handed pitcher of all time, and I'm honored to be his friend and teammate.

My pitching motion, seen here from start to finish, has to stay consistent on every pitch from the start of spring training until the final out of the season.

PITCHING
WITH
YOUR MIND

The mind has an incredible influence on sports performance. The smallest thing can alter your ability to focus on your job. It could be a mistake pitch you made to a hitter. It could be an off-the-field distraction, where something is bothering you and it creeps into your mind when you are pitching.

I'm blessed with the ability to throw a 98-mph fastball, and have benefited from working with a Hall of Fame pitcher like Nolan Ryan, but would I have achieved so much success without the mental focus that goes with me every time I take the mound?

I've been able to dig deep within myself to produce an almost callous, stone-faced approach to my craft. This stern mentality has worked for me, but it isn't something that works for every pitcher. The point is that you must find something within yourself to motivate you and push you past your physical limits.

Conventional wisdom dictates that certain athletes are better than others at dealing with pressure. The mind has a lot to do with how you cope with pressure, and for that matter so does your heart. It is up to you to realize that baseball is not a life-and-death situation. But that does not mean you should rationalize away any failure. Learn from your mistakes and use your mind to help you not to repeat them.

I've been playing this game since I was seven years old. I don't know how much longer I will pitch, and that's a funny feeling, because baseball has been my whole life. When I was a little boy, it was fun. I've matured, turned it into a profession, and I'm still having fun.

But when I'm done with the game, it is final—the umbilical cord is cut. I can no longer go through the routines that have been so much a part of my life for so long. That first spring training after retirement will be an odd experience. I won't be playing catch the day after Christmas to prepare for spring training. What will I do?

I've put time and hard work into my career, and the day will come when I no longer can analyze everything to see how I can get better, because the time to do that will no longer exist.

I know many athletes view retirement with mixed feelings. The thing that's missing is the competition you have had your entire life. That's what I prepare for. And that sense of competitive purpose is what I will miss most.

If you want to be the best, you have to set yourself apart from the rest. It sounds so simple, but it is the truth. I've taken my talent to another level by never getting complacent.

Tiger Woods is a great golfer. He has a gift. But there's so much more to his success than his raw ability to hit a golf ball. His approach to the game is what sets him apart from the pack.

Regardless of what I have achieved—all the records and the awards—until my final hour as a baseball player I will continue to work to get better at what I do.

My advice to young pitchers is to adhere to a steady routine of physical conditioning, consistent mechanics, mental intensity, and complete focus on success. Once you enjoy success, high expectations will follow, and that's a double-edged sword. On the one hand, you want to be counted on by your teammates as a money pitcher; on the other, it isn't much fun to have your success taken for granted and accepted as a given.

Don't let success take the fun out of your achievements in baseball. Follow the example of my career, and the practical information on power pitching to push your natural talent to its outer limits. And most of all, remember that baseball is a game, and the enjoyment that goes with playing that game must come first before you can achieve your ultimate potential.

My record-setting twenty strikeout performance against the Cincinnati Reds on May 8, 2001.

Appendix A

THE R.J. ALL-TIME STRIKEOUT LIST (3,412)*

Jeff Abbott 1	Skeeter Barnes 5	Wade Boggs 8
Kurt Abbott 9	Michael Barrett 1	Barry Bonds 5
Shawn Abner 4	Jeff Barry 3	Bobby Bonilla 4
Bobby Abreu 2	Kimera Bartee 1	Aaron Boone 3
Benny Agbayani 3	Kevin Bass 2	Bret Boone 8
Luis Aguayo 1	Jason Bates 2	Pat Borders 10
Manny Alexander . . . 9	Justin Baughman 3	Mike Bordick 11
Edgardo Alfonzo 3	Danny Bautista 2	Kent Bottenfield 1
Luis Alicea 2	Rich Becker 6	Rafael Bournigal 1
Andy Allanson 6	Derek Bell 7	Jim Bowic 1
Roberto Alomar 12	George A. Bell 3	Milton Bradley 5
Sandy Alomar Jr. 4	Jay Bell 8	Phil Bradley 4
Moises Alou 1	Albert Belle 16	Darren Bragg 2
Ruben Amaro Jr. 1	Mark Bellhorn 5	Glenn Braggs 2
Brady Anderson 13	Rafael Belliard 1	Sid Bream 2
Garret Anderson 6	Carlos Beltran 1	George Brett 5
Jimmy Anderson 2	Adrian Beltre 9	Tilson Brito 4
Shane Andrews 6	Esteban Beltre 6	Bernardo Britto 1
Rick Ankiel 1	Mike Benjamin 4	Rico Brogna 6
Alex Arias 6	Gary Bennett 1	Hubie Brooks 4
George Arias 3	Jason Bere 3	Scott Brosius 7
Tony R. Armas 2	Dave Berg 5	Bob Brower 1
Jack Armstrong 1	Lance Berkman 3	Adrian Brown 4
Andy Ashby 2	Geronimo Berroa 6	Emil Brown 4
Pedro Astacio 1	Sean Berry 3	Kevin Brown 2
Rich Aurilia 7	Dante Bichette 11	Kevin L. Brown 2
Bruce Aven 3	Craig Biggio 3	Roosevelt Brown 1
Carlos Baerga 7	Henry Blanco 3	Jerry Browne 4
Jeff Bagwell 4	Lance Blankenship . . 4	Cliff Brumbaugh 1
Steve Balboni 4	Jeff Blauser 4	Jacob Brumfield 1
Bret Barberie 1	Mike Blowers 2	Tom Brunansky 12
Jesse Barfield 3	Geoff Blum 5	Steve Buechele 3
Glen Barker 1	Hiram Bocachica 2	Damon Buford 7

*As of the end of the 2001 baseball season

115

Greg Gagne ○ ○ ○ ○ ○ ○ ○ 17
Andres Galarraga ○ ○ ○ ○ 9
Dave Gallagher ○ ○ ○ ○ ○ 1
Mike Gallego ○ ○ ○ ○ ○ ○ ○ 5
Ron Gant ○ ○ ○ ○ ○ ○ ○ ○ 12
Jim Gantner ○ ○ ○ ○ ○ ○ ○ 1
Carlos Garcia ○ ○ ○ ○ ○ ○ 2
Freddy Garcia ○ ○ ○ ○ ○ ○ 3
Nomar Garciaparra ○ ○ ○ 7
Mark Gardner ○ ○ ○ ○ ○ ○ 2
Daniel Garibay ○ ○ ○ ○ ○ ○ 1
Brent Gates ○ ○ ○ ○ ○ ○ ○ 8
Bob Geren ○ ○ ○ ○ ○ ○ ○ ○ 1
Jason Giambi ○ ○ ○ ○ ○ ○ ○ 1
Kirk Gibson ○ ○ ○ ○ ○ ○ ○ 3
Benji Gil ○ ○ ○ ○ ○ ○ ○ ○ ○ 10
Shawn Gilbert ○ ○ ○ ○ ○ ○ 3
Brian Giles ○ ○ ○ ○ ○ ○ ○ ○ 8
Joe Girardi ○ ○ ○ ○ ○ ○ ○ ○ 6
Dan Gladden ○ ○ ○ ○ ○ ○ ○ 5
Doug Glanville ○ ○ ○ ○ ○ 7
Troy Glaus ○ ○ ○ ○ ○ ○ ○ ○ 2
Tom Glavine ○ ○ ○ ○ ○ ○ ○ 9
Chris Gomez ○ ○ ○ ○ ○ ○ ○ 5
Leo Gomez ○ ○ ○ ○ ○ ○ ○ ○ 7
Alex Gonzalez ○ ○ ○ ○ ○ ○ 2
Jose Gonzalez ○ ○ ○ ○ ○ ○ ○ 1
Juan Gonzalez ○ ○ ○ ○ ○ 16
Luis Gonzalez ○ ○ ○ ○ ○ ○ ○ 3
Rene Gonzalez ○ ○ ○ ○ ○ ○ 2
Wiki Gonzalez ○ ○ ○ ○ ○ ○ 3
Curtis Goodwin ○ ○ ○ ○ ○ 4
Tom Goodwin ○ ○ ○ ○ ○ ○ ○ 8
Mark Grace ○ ○ ○ ○ ○ ○ ○ 3
Craig Grebeck ○ ○ ○ ○ ○ ○ 5
Scarborough Green ○ ○ 3
Shawn Green ○ ○ ○ ○ ○ ○ ○ 6
Mike Greenwell ○ ○ ○ ○ ○ 4
Rusty Greer ○ ○ ○ ○ ○ ○ ○ 8
Ben Grieve ○ ○ ○ ○ ○ ○ ○ ○ 1
Ken Griffey Jr. ○ ○ ○ ○ ○ ○ 1
Marquis Grissom ○ ○ ○ 15
Kelly Gruber ○ ○ ○ ○ ○ ○ ○ 5
Mark Grudzielanek ○ ○ 11
Pedro Guerrero ○ ○ ○ ○ ○ 2

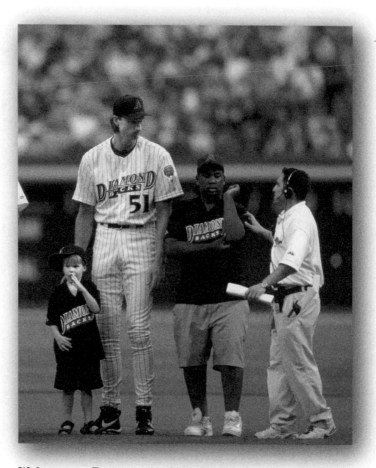

With my son Tanner at the 2000 All-Star Game in Atlanta.

Vladimir Guerrero ○ ○ ○ 6
Wilton Guerrero ○ ○ ○ ○ ○ 2
Jose Guillen ○ ○ ○ ○ ○ ○ ○ 7
Ozzie Guillen ○ ○ ○ ○ ○ ○ ○ 5
Jackie Gutierrez ○ ○ ○ ○ ○ 1
Ricky Gutierrez ○ ○ ○ ○ ○ 2
Tony Gwynn ○ ○ ○ ○ ○ ○ ○ ○ 4
Shane Halter ○ ○ ○ ○ ○ ○ ○ 9
Darryl Hamilton ○ ○ ○ ○ ○ 3
Jeffrey Hammonds ○ ○ 11
Mike Hampton ○ ○ ○ ○ ○ ○ 1
Mike Harkey ○ ○ ○ ○ ○ ○ ○ 2
Brian Harper ○ ○ ○ ○ ○ ○ ○ 5
Donald Harris ○ ○ ○ ○ ○ ○ 4
Bill Haselman ○ ○ ○ ○ ○ ○ 3

Billy Hatcher ○ ○ ○ ○ ○ ○ ○ 5
Scott Hatteberg ○ ○ ○ ○ ○ 1
Charlie Hayes ○ ○ ○ ○ ○ ○ 5
Mike Heath ○ ○ ○ ○ ○ ○ ○ ○ 3
Wes Helms ○ ○ ○ ○ ○ ○ ○ ○ 3
Todd Helton ○ ○ ○ ○ ○ ○ ○ 2
Scott Hemond ○ ○ ○ ○ ○ ○ 11
Dave Henderson ○ ○ ○ ○ ○ 9
Rickey Henderson ○ ○ ○ 28
Pat Hentgen ○ ○ ○ ○ ○ ○ ○ 2
Carlos A. Hernandez ○ ○ 1
Jose Hernandez ○ ○ ○ ○ ○ 10
Ramon Hernandez ○ ○ ○ 3
Phil Hiatt ○ ○ ○ ○ ○ ○ ○ ○ 5
Richard Hidalgo ○ ○ ○ ○ 4

Making a pitch at the 1993 All-Star game.

Jeff Kent 11	Torey Lovullo 2	Brian Meadows 1
Darryl Kile 4	Mike Lowell 5	Pat Mears 12
Jeff King 3	Julio Lugo 4	Luis Medina 2
Ron Kittle 4	Scott Lydy 4	Dave Meier 1
Chuck Knoblauch 10	Kevin Maas 4	Adam Melhuse 1
Randy Knorr 1	Mike Macfarlane 14	Mitch Melusky 1
Brad Komminsk 3	Shane Mack 13	Bob Melvin 6
Mark Kotsay 2	Greg Maddux 1	Donaldo Mendez 3
Chad Kreuter 9	Pat Mahomes 2	Frank Menechino 3
Jeff Kunkel 7	Candy Maldonado 9	Henry Mercedes 2
Tim Laker 1	Fred Manrique 5	Luis Mercedes 1
Tom Lampkin 3	Jeff Manto 9	Hensley Meulens 4
Carney Lansford 1	Kirt Manwaring 3	Chad Meyers 2
Mike Lansing 7	Eli Marrero 6	Matt Mieske 3
Dave LaPoint 1	Mike A. Marshall 1	Kevin Millar 6
Barry Larkin 6	Norberto Martin 4	Keith A. Miller 4
Jason LaRue 3	Carlos Martinez 5	Randy Milligan 3
Tim Laudner 2	Carmelo Martinez 1	Doug Mirabelli 2
Tom Lawless 2	Dave Martinez 4	Kevin Mitchell 3
Brian Lawrence 1	Domingo Martinez 2	Bengie Molina 1
Aaron Ledesma 4	Edgar Martinez 1	Paul Molitor 10
Derreck Lee 9	Felix Martinez 2	Raul Mondesi 3
Manuel Lee 8	Manny Martinez 6	Mickey Morandini 1
Al Leiter 1	Ramon E. Martinez 1	Mike Mordecai 3
Scott Leius 4	Tino Martinez 1	Keith Moreland 1
Mark Lemke 2	John Marzano 1	Lloyd Moseby 2
Chet Lemon 1	Damon Mashore 3	James Mouton 8
Patrick Lennon 3	Mike Matheny 13	Lyle Mouton 8
Jesse Levis 1	Gary Matthews Jr. 8	Bill Mueller 2
Darren Lewis 5	Don Mattingly 2	Pedro Munoz 13
Mark Lewis 4	Brent Mayne 2	Dale Murphy 2
Jim Leyritz 24	Dave McCarty 9	Calvin Murray 5
Jon Lieber 2	Scott McClain 2	Eddie Murray 1
Mike Lieberthal 6	Quinton McCracken 5	Greg Myers 2
Jose Lind 2	Rodney McCray 2	Rodney Myers 1
Nelson Liriano 1	Jason McDonald 4	Tim Naehring 8
Pat Listach 8	Oddibe McDowell 3	Denny Neagle 1
Mark Little 6	Joe McEwing 4	Troy Neel 3
Paul Lo Duca 4	Willie McGee 2	Phil Nevin 16
Kenny Lofton 12	Fred McGriff 2	Marc Newfield 2
Ryan Long 2	Mark McGwire 18	Al Newman 4
Javy Lopez 8	Tony McKnight 1	Jose Nieves 3
Luis Lopez 1	Mark McLemore 10	Melvin Nieves 8
Mendy Lopez 2	Brian McRae 9	David Nillson 2
Mark Loretta 10	Kevin McReynolds 4	Otis Nixon 8

It was a highlight to join Roger Clemens and Kerry Wood as the only pitchers to strike out twenty in a nine-inning span.

John Kruk, then of the Philadelphia Phillies and a great hitter, was always fun to compete against.

Appendix B

RANDY JOHNSON'S MINOR- AND MAJOR-LEAGUE PITCHING TOTALS

YEAR	CLUB	W–L	ERA	G	GS	CG	SHO	SV	IP	H	R	ER	BB	SO
1985	Jamestown	0–3	5.93	8	8	0	0	0	27.1	29	22	18	24	21
1986	West Palm Beach	8–7	3.16	26	26	2	1	0	119.2	89	49	42	94	133
1987	Jacksonville	11–8	3.73	25	24	0	0	0	140.0	100	63	58	128	163
1988	Indianapolis	8–7	3.26	20	19	0	0	0	113.1	85	52	41	2	111
	Montreal	3–0	2.42	4	4	1	0	0	26.0	23	8	7	7	25
1989	Montreal	0–4	6.67	7	6	0	0	0	29.2	29	25	22	26	26
	Indianapolis	1–1	2.00	3	3	0	0	0	18.0	13	5	4	9	17
	Seattle	7–9	4.40	22	22	2	0	0	131.0	118	75	64	70	104
1990	Seattle	14–11	3.65	33	33	5	2	0	219.2	174	103	89	120	194
1991	Seattle	13–10	3.98	33	33	2	1	0	201.1	151	96	89	152	241
1992	Seattle	12–14	3.77	31	31	6	2	0	210.1	154	104	88	144	241
1993	Seattle	19–8	3.24	35	34	10	3	1	255.1	185	97	92	99	308
1994	Seattle	13–6	3.19	23	23	9	4	0	172.0	132	65	61	72	204
1995	Seattle	18–2	2.48	30	30	6	3	0	214.1	159	65	59	65	294
1996	Seattle	5–0	3.67	14	8	0	0	1	61.1	48	27	25	25	85
	Everett*	0–0	0.00	1	1	0	0		2.0	0	0	0	0	5
1997	Seattle	20–4	2.28	30	29	5	2	0	213.0	147	60	54	77	291
1998	Seattle	9–10	4.33	23	23	6	2	0	160.0	146	90	77	60	213
	Houston	10–1	1.28	11	11	4	4	0	84.1	57	12	12	26	116
1999	Arizona	17–9	2.48	35	35	12	2	0	271.2	207	86	75	70	364
2000	Arizona	19–7	2.64	35	35	8	3	0	248.2	202	89	73	76	347
2001	Arizona	21–6	2.49	35	34	3	2	0	249.2	181	74	69	71	372
AL Totals		130–74	3.42	274	266	51	19	2	1838.1	1414	782	698	884	2162
NL Totals		70–27	2.55	127	125	18	11	0	909.1	699	294	258	276	1250
ML Totals		200–101	3.13	401	391	69	30	2	2747.2	2113	1076	956	1160	3412

*Minor league injury rehab.

Division Series Record

YEAR	CLUB	W–L	ERA	G	GS	CG	SHO	SV	IP	H	R	ER	BB	SO
1995	Sea. vs. N.Y.	2–0	2.70	2	1	0	0	0	10.0	5	3	3	6	16
1997	Sea. vs. Balt.	0–2	5.54	2	2	1	0	0	13.0	14	8	8	6	16
1998	Hou. vs. S.D.	0–2	1.93	2	2	0	0	0	14.0	12	4	3	2	17
1999	Az. vs. N.Y.	0–1	7.56	1	1	0	0	0	8.1	8	7	7	3	11
2001	Az. vs. St. L.	0–1	3.38	1	1	0	0	0	8.0	6	3	3	2	9
Division Series Totals		2–6	4.05	8	7	1	0	0	53.1	45	25	24	19	69

League Championship Series

YEAR	CLUB	W–L	ERA	G	GS	CG	SHO	SV	IP	H	R	ER	BB	SO
1995	Sea. vs. Clev.	0–1	2.35	2	2	0	0	0	15.1	12	6	4	2	13
2001	Az. vs. Atl.	2–0	1.13	2	2	1	1	0	16.0	10	2	2	3	19
LCS Totals		2–1	2.30	4	4	1	1	0	31.1	22	8	6	5	32

World Series Record

YEAR	CLUB	W–L	ERA	G	GS	CG	SHO	SV	IP	H	R	ER	BB	SO
2001	Az. vs. N.Y.	3–0	1.04	3	2	1	1	0	17.1	9	2	2	3	19

All-Star Game Record

YEAR	CLUB	W–L	ERA	G	GS	CG	SHO	SV	IP	H	R	ER	BB	SO
1990	AL @ Chi.			Did not pitch.										
1993	AL @ Balt.	0–0	0.00	1	0	0	0	0	2.0	0	0	0	0	1
1994	AL @ Pitt.	0–0	9.00	1	0	0	0	0	1.0	2	1	1	0	0
1995	AL @ Texas	0–0	0.00	1	1	0	0	0	2.0	0	0	0	1	3
1997	AL @ Cleve.	0–0	0.00	1	1	0	0	0	2.0	0	0	0	1	2
1999	NL @ Bos.	0–0	0.00	1	0	0	0	0	1.0	0	0	0	0	1
2000	NL @ Atl.	0–0	0.00	1	1	0	0	0	1.0	1	0	0	0	1
2001	NL @ Sea.	0–0	0.00	1	1	0	0	0	2.0	1	0	0	0	3
All-Star Game Totals		0–0	0.82	7	4	0	0	0	11.0	4	1	1	2	11

Checking out the starting lineup with AL skipper Joe Torre at the 1997 All-Star Game.

Randy's Career Bests

Season

Wins ○○ 21, 2001
ERA ○○○ 2.28, 2001
Strikeouts ○○○○○○○○○○○○○○○○○○○○○○○○○○○○○○○○○○○○○○○ 372, 2001
Winning Streak ○○○○○○○○○○○○○○○○○○○○ 8 games, twice (last: 2001)

Single Games

Strikeouts, Starter ○○○○○○○○○○○○ 20 vs. Cincinnati, May 8, 2001
Strikeouts, Reliever ○○○○○○○○○○○ 16 @ San Diego, July 18, 2001
Low-Hit Game ○○○○○○○○○○○ No-hitter vs. Detroit, June 2, 1990

Randy Johnson's Foundation

The Randy D. Johnson Foundation, a National Heritage Foundation, was founded by Randy and his wife, Lisa, in 2000. The purpose of his foundation is to assist children and families in economic need in realizing their full potential.

The foundation has donated to organizations like the American Red Cross, the Cystic Fibrosis Foundation, and many homeless and children's organizations.

To make donations to the Randy D. Johnson Foundation, please call Kimberly Morton at 847-583-2070 or write to:

The Randy D. Johnson Foundation
A National Heritage Foundation
c/o CSMG
5215 Old Orchard Road
Suite 1000
Skokie, IL 60077